Miscellaneous Cherokee and Choctaw Records 1800-1900

Bob Curry

HERITAGE BOOKS
2008

HERITAGE BOOKS
AN IMPRINT OF HERITAGE BOOKS, INC.

Books, CDs, and more—Worldwide

For our listing of thousands of titles see our website
at
www.HeritageBooks.com

Published 2008 by
HERITAGE BOOKS, INC.
Publishing Division
100 Railroad Ave. #104
Westminster, Maryland 21157

Copyright © 2001 Bob Curry

Other books by Bob Curry and K.M. Armstrong:
Chickasaw Rolls: Annuity Rolls of 1857-1860 & the "1855" Chickasaw District Roll of 1856,

All rights reserved. No part of this book may be reproduced or transmitted in any form or by any means, electronic or mechanical, including photocopying, recording or by any information storage and retrieval system without written permission from the author, except for the inclusion of brief quotations in a review.

International Standard Book Numbers
Paperbound: 978-0-7884-1912-6
Clothbound: 978-0-7884-7073-8

Table of Contents

Introduction	v
About The Author	vii
Eastern Cherokee Annuity Roll of 1871	1
Choctaw Nation – Schools (1800s to 1900s) "A list of Choctaw Indians Educated in the States" by Peter J. Hudson	6
Cyrus Byington's List of Choctaw Soldiers, Civil War	25
Hocha's Settlement	26
Men Remaining	26
The Other Company	27
Soldiers	27
Choctaw Roll: 1856	28
Rhoda Pitchlynn Howell's Bible Records	39
Index	41

Introduction

The genealogy researcher knows that every little bit of information is important to finding a family history connection. I would like to make these pieces of genealogical information available to all Indian researchers. This book contains transcribed payment rolls for the Cherokee and Choctaw Indian Nations. Within these pages are rolls which have never before been formally published or listed as published works. To provide additional information for research and genealogical study, I have included the 1871 Eastern Cherokee Annuity Roll, the 1856 Choctaw Annuity Roll, a list of Choctaw students educated in the States, Choctaw Civil War soldiers and the transcribed Bible records from Rhoda Pitchlynn's lost Bible. The Indian rolls are the transcribed copies of the originals kept by the Bureau of Indian Affairs in Washington DC. As many Choctaw researchers are aware, the Pitchlynns were a prominent and influential pioneer Choctaw family in Indian Territory.

Generally, the annuity rolls were used by the Government to record and keep track of payments made to Indian families. We would appreciate your assistance in helping us to identify the English names of those Indians who appear on the annuity rolls under their Indian names. We hope that these pieces of genealogy information will help you complete your family search.

February, 2001
Bobby R. Curry

About The Author

Bob Curry is a graduate of Oklahoma Baptist University (1974) and East Central University (1995). He has a Bachelor and a Master's Degree in History and Human Resources. Bob has authored several historical articles and genealogical works. Mr. Curry, along with Mr. Kerry Armstrong, was a contributing author to the *"Chickasaw Annuity Rolls (1855 to 1860)."* In addition, Mr. Curry has written several published and unpublished genealogical works, i.e.; *"The Princes of the Blood," "The Bethlehem Cemetery Records," "My Beloved Brother, Thomas Jefferson Pitchlynn," "The Bruner Family Records," "The Curry Family-Alabama Mulattos (1840 to 1990)"* and *"The Pitchlynns, a synopsis of Peter Pitchlynn's letters."*

Eastern Cherokee Annuity Roll of 1871

We the undersigned Eastern or North Carolina Cherokee Indians do hereby acknowledge to have received by from the United States by the hand of John B. Jones, US Indian Agent, the sums opposite our names in full payment of our share of the per capita fund of $53.33 and the interest due therein, provided by the Act of July 29, 1848, in commutation for removal and subsistence for those Cherokees who have removed themselves to the nation west of the Mississippi.

Name of Claimants & heirs	Miller Roll no.	Sex & age	immigrated	Amount per Capita	Interest	Total
A-na-soo-yah or Mix Water	31	M 50	1867	$53.33	$7.73	$61.06
Oo-yas-ke-wah-tah	665	M 61	1867	$53.33	39.73	93.06
Ka-ta-ih (wife) died in 1868	666	F	1867	$53.33	39.73	93.06
Two orphan children Dah-hah & Cha-wa-louge		F 18 & M 8				
How-a-qrua, or Eth, Died 1869	829		1867			
Susan (wife) died in N. Carolina	830					
Susan's heirs: Songster		M 14		$21.34	13.76	35.10
Susan's heirs: Falling Flower		M 12		$21.33	13.76	35.09
Susan's heir: Josiah		M 10		$21.33	13.76	35.09
Susan's heir: Telala		F 7		$21.33	13.75	35.08
Susan's heir: Ahlasih In N.C.		F 20		$21.33	3.09	24.42
Betsy Davis (Widow) Heirs: Thomas Monroe Neppa George	996	F 63 M 11 M 9 M 7 M 5	1856	$53.33	39.73	93.06
Sarah Henson (wife of A. Smith Heirs: Mary Jane McDormat	1007		1854	$53.33	39.73	93.06
J. L. A. Smith	1057	36	1855	$53.33	39.73	93.06
Nancy Ann Tinson	1063	43	1849	$53.33	39.73	93.06
John C. Tinson	1063	40	1854	$53.33	39.73	93.06
Eliza Tinson (wife of A.Bur) died 1869 Heirs: Melvina Franklin Ah-gua-tah	1065	F 12 M 10 F 6	1854	$17.78 $17.78 $ 17.78	13.24 13.24 13.25	31.02 31.02 31.02

Names of Claimants & Heirs	Miller roll no.	Sex/Age	Immigrated	Per Capita	Interest	Total
H. Clay **Tinson**	1066	M 36	1854	$53.33	$39.73	$93.06
Martha Jane **Tinson** (wife of J. Arnold died: 1866 (Heirs) Thomas William Lucy	1067	13 9 4	1854	$17.78 17.78 17.78	$13.24 13.24 13.24	$31.02 31.02 31.02
Edward **Welch** (died: 1867) Heirs: Laura **Taylor** in N.C. Ellen D. **Phillips** Alfred **Welch** Mary **Welch** George **Welch** Richard **Welch** (I.T.) Ada **McKee** (I.T.) John **Welch** (Texas)	1463		1867	$6.67 Same " " " " "	$.97 Same " " " " "	$7.64 Same " " " " "
Richard **Welch**	1461			$53.33	$17.75	$71.06
David **Welch** (died 1855) (Heirs) John **Welch** Medora **Welch** **Welch**	1464	23 18 16	1853	$17.78 $17.78 $17.78	$13.24 $13.24 $13.25	$31.02 $31.02 $31.02
James **Welch** (Heirs): **Haston** John C Cornelia	1465	47 20 17 15	1867	$53.33	$39.73	$93.06
Lucy Te-Sus-Ke	942			$53.33	$39.73	$93.06
Achela or Rachel Tah-gah-do-gak	149			$53.33	$7.73	$61.06
Wilson **Jek-hin-nih**	1486	43	1867	$53.33	$39.73	$93.06
Charles **Raper** (heirs) Julia Ann **Wallace**	1039		1834			

Roll of payments to be made by J.B. Jones, U.S. Indian Agent embracing the names of the North Carolina or Eastern Cherokee Indians, who were removed west under the supervision of Majors Lang and Cox in 1871, and are entitled, as original claimants or heirs of those who have deceased, to the per capita fund of $53.33 and accrued interest, as provided by the act of July 29th 1848:

No	Name	Roll No	Sex	Age	Miller roll	Entitled	Share	Per Capita	Time	Interest	Total
1	Te-sa-ni-hih	864	M	45	793 792 794 795	Self Mother Brother Sister	All	$53.33	3/92	$8.80	$62.13 $62.13 $62.13 $62.13
2	Susy (wife)	865	F	41	68 69 258	Father Mother Brother	1/8	$6.67 $6.66 $6.67		$1.00 $1.00 $1.00	$7.77 $7.76 $7.77
3	Sa-la-nih (daughter)	866	F	13							$25.00
4	Wa-ti-nih**Error! Bookmark not defined.**	867	F	10							$25.00
5	Ju-na-lus-kih	868	M	8							$25.00
6	Smith	869	M	4							$25.00
7	Sah-ne-co-yah	334	M	48	911	Self	All	$53.33	3/72	$8.80	$62.63

8	Lucy (wife)	835	F	37	838	Do	All	$53.33	"	$8.80	$62.63
					836	Sister	All	$53.33		$8.80	$62.13
					784	Father	¾	$40.00		$6.60	$46.60
					1376	G-father	All	$53.33		$8.80	$62.13
					1377	Aunt	All	$53.33		$8.80	$62.13
9	Ta-la-tes-skih (Son)	836	M	13							$25.00
10	Charley (Son)	837	M	11							$25.00
11	Lydia (daughter)	838	F	9							$25.00
12	Ah-ni-nie (son)	839	M	7							$25.00
13	William (Son)	840	M	5							$25.00
14	Te-la-gus-kih (Son)	841	M	4							$25.00
15	Ezekiel	1086	M	46	791		¾	$40.00	3/72	$6.60	$46.60
					762	Sister	¾	$40.00		$6.60	$46.60
					763	Cousin	all	$53.33		$8.80	$62.13
					1498	Mother	all	$53.33		$8.80	$62.13
16	Linda or Kyo-hawk-kah (wife)	1087	F	39							$25.00
17	Nice (daughter)	1088	F	15							$25.00
18	Sally (daughter)	1089	F	13							$25.00
19	Tah-nih (daughter)	1090	F	10							$25.00
20	Ellek (son)	1091	M	8							$25.00
21	Sul-te-she (son)	1092	M	7							$25.00
22	Che-ah-sa-hi (daughter)	1093	F	5							$25.00
23	Oo-ne-tah-tah	1081	M	51	882	Self	All	$53.33	3/72	$8.27	$62.13
					883	Wife	All	$53.33		$8.83	$62.13
					872	Gfather	1/8	$6.67		$1.13	$7.77
24	Skinn-ta-hih (son)	1083	M	19							$25.00
25	Nancy (daughter)	1085	F	7							$25.00
26	Ahl-sih	804	F	35							$70.00
27	Joe Locust	910	M	68	863	Self	All	$53.33	3/72	$8.80	$62.13
					866	Son	All	$53.33		$8.80	$62.13
					867	Daughter	All	$53.33		$8.80	$62.13
					1268	Uncle	1/3	$17.78		$2.93	$20.73
					1266	Uncle	1/3	$17.77		$2.94	$20.71
					1267	Cousin	1/3	$17.78		$2.94	$20.71
					1234	Uncle	1/4	$13.33		$2.27	$15.53
28	Cul-stih-yih (wife)	911	F	66	864	Self	All	$53.33	3/72	$2.27	$62.13
					832	Mother	All	$53.33		$8.87	$62.13
					1255	Gmother	All	$53.33		$8.87	$62.13
					1354	Cousin	1/3	$17.78		$2.93	$20.71
					1355	Cousin	1/3	$17.77		$2.94	$20.71
					1356	Cousin	1/3	$17.78		$2.93	$20.71
					1446	Neice	All	$53.33		$8.87	$62.13
					1494	Uncle	All	$53.33		$8.87	$62.63
29	Che-ca-yu-eh (Daughter)	912	F	24							$25.00
30	Louisa (Daughter of Che-ca-yu-eh)	913	F	4							$25.00
31	No-hoo-lah (son of Joe Locust)	914	M	23							$25.00
32	Martha (daughter)	915	F	15							$25.00
33	Jessie Locust (son)	916	M	22							$25.00

#	Name	ID	Sex	Age	ID2	Relation	Share	Amount	Date	Fee	Total
34	Sally (Jessie's wife)	917	F	21							$25.00
35	Chu-ga-lees-kili (wife of Augusta, son of Joe Locust)	924	F	25							$25.00
36	Ah-lih	857	F	49	788	Self	All	$53.33	3/72	$8.87	$62.13
					966	Gmother	All	$53.33		$8.87	$62.13
					868	Brother	¼	$13.33		$2.27	$15.53
					848	Husband	All	$53.33		$8.87	$62.13
					1276	Uncle	1/2	$26.67		$4.40	$31.07
37	James (son)	858	M	19							$25.00
38	Martin (son)	860	M	10							$25.00
39	Wah-che-soh (son)	861	M	6							$25.00
40	Wah-ka-nih (daughter)	862	F	5							$25.00
41	Ache-lik or Rachel	327	F	56	726	Self	All	$53.33	3/72	$8.87	$62.00
					15	Husband	1/3	$53.33		$8.80	$62.00
					724	Father	1/3	$17.78		$2.93	$20.70
					727	Sister	1/3	$17.77		$2.94	$20.70
					128	Brother	1/3	$17.78		$2.93	$20.70
					748	Uncle	1/3	$17.77		$2.94	$20.70
					1274	G-father	1/3	$17.78		$2.93	$20.70
					747	Mother	All	$53.33		$8.87	$62.00
42	Co-wa-la-skih	822	M	67	782	Self	All	$53.33	3/72	$8.80	$62.00
					822	Father	½	$26.67		$4.40	$31.00
					98	Sister	½	$26.67		$4.40	$31.00
					1402	Aunt	½	$26.66		$4.40	$31.00
					1403	Bro-in-law	½	$26.66		$4.40	$31.00
					1274	Uncle	1/3	$17.78		$2.93	$20.00
43	Ce-lih (wife)	823	F	52	783	Self	All	$53.33	3/72	$8.80	$62.00
					790	Mother	¼	$13.34		$2.20	$15.00
					873	Brother	¼	$13.33		$2.20	$15.00
					909	Uncle	¼	$13.33		$2.20	$15.00
					770	Sister	¼	$13.33		$2.20	$15.00
44	Newton (son)	827	M	18							
45	Carter (son)	828	M	15							
46	Ce-ca-we (Daughter)	830	F	10							
47	Charlotte (daughter)	831	F	8							
48	Julia (Granddaughter)	833	F	4							
49	Peter (son)	825	M	22							
50	Tua-ka-aya (wife of Peter)	826	F	20							
51	Ellan-a-you-na-cah	49	M	47	1382	Self	All	$53.33	3/72	$8.89	$62.00
					1389	Aunt	1/6	$8.89		$1.46	$10.00
					1098	Cousin	1/6	$8.89		$1.47	$10.00
52	Betsy (wife)	50	F	28							
					1148		1/6	$8.89		$1.46	$10.00
					115		1/6	$26.67		$4.40	$31.00
					35		1/6	$8.89		$1.47	$10.00
53	John Larcky (son)	51	M	4							
54	John Arka-loo-ka	788	M	55	685	Self	All	$53.33	3/72	$8.80	$62.00
					615	Sister	1/3	$17.78		$2.95	$20.00
					616	Brother	1/3	$17.77		$2.95	$20.00
55	Wesley (son)	792	M	13							
56	? M Henson	1232	F	78	1002	Self	All	$53.33	3/72	$8.80	
					1001	Husband	2/11	$9.69		$1.60	
					1004	Daughter	All	$53.33		$8.80	
					1005	Daughter	2/11	$9.70		$1.60	
					1396	Cousin	1/3	$17.78		$2.93	
					1050	Mother	1/3	$17.77		$2.93	

57	Rebecca (daughter)	1247	F	54	1053	Self Father Sister	All	$53.33		$8.80 $.80 $.80	
58	William **Henson**	1248	M	42	1003 1001 1005	Self Father Sister	All 1/11 1/11	$53.33	3/72	$8.80 $ .80 $ .80	
59	Benjamin (descendant)	1249	M	35	1001 1005		1/11 1/11	$4.85 $4.85		$ .80 $ .80	
60	Thomas (Do)	1250	M	32							
61	Judah (Do)	1252		19							
62	William (Do)	1253	M	16							
63	Charley (Do)	1254	M	13							
64	Scott (Do)	1255	M	10							
65	Richard (Do)	1256	M	6							
66	John (Do)	1257	M	4							
67	Kinn (Do)	1258	M	12							
68	Thomas (Do)	1259	M	7							
69	Pearle (Do)	1260	F	5							
70	Mary (Do)	1266	F	15							
71	Dilly (Do)	1265	F	10							
72	Jack (Do)	1263	M	4							

22521-A
Choctaw Nation- Schools (1800s to 1900s)
Students in the States
"A list of Choctaw Indians Educated in the States,"
By Peter J. Hudson
(This information is located at the Indian Archives, Okla. City, OK)

Name of Student	Year	Name of School
Adams, John Quincy Bn: 1824	1832	Choctaw Academy, Teacher at Betha-bara
Allen, Samuel	1832	Choctaw Academy in Kentucky
Auston, John	1832	Choctaw Academy in Kentucky
Adams, Mitchell C.- son of William C. Adams	1870	Spencer Academy, Indian Terr
Ainsworth, Thomas D.		No notations or information
Ainsworth, Napoleon B- son J.G. Ainsworth	1870	Spencer Academy & Roanoke College; Clerk for Representative 1877
Ainsworth, Jessie- daughter of Thomas D Ainsworth		Baird College, Clinton, MO.
Ainsworth, James	1886-87	No notation or other information
Adams, Missie		St. Agnes, Antlers, Oklahoma
Appliton, Jesse		Mission School, Mississippi
Battiest, Fransaway	1832	Choctaw Academy; Supreme Judge 1863; member of Skullyville Constitutional Convention
Baxter, Richard		Choctaw Academy, Kentucky
Barbour, James		Choctaw Academy, Kentucky
Birch, Sampson		Choctaw Academy, Kentucky
Black, James D.		Choctaw Academy, Kentucky
Brewer, Elijah		Son of Nukpullichvbbi 1881
Brewer, James	1836	Choctaw Academy, Kentucky; Teacher at Betha-Bara 1836
Bryant, William		Choctaw Academy, KY; Delegate to Creek Convention 1861; Supreme Judge 1865; Chief
Burris, Gabriel	1832	Choctaw Academy, KY; Supreme Judge 1863 & 1865
Breashears, Charley		Choctaw Academy, Kentucky
Brandan, J. C.	Bn 1818	Choctaw Academy, Kentucky
Brainard, Millard		Choctaw Academy, Kentucky
Brainard, Thomas born 1816	1832	Choctaw Academy, Kentucky
Brown, Silas		Choctaw Academy, Kentucky

Buckhold, August	Bn 1814	Choctaw Academy, Kentucky
Byington, Jerrymiah	Bn 1811	Choctaw Academy, Kentucky
Byington, Thomas H.	1874	Blue County
Belvin, Watson J.		Bennington, Oklahoma
Brown, Myrtle	1896	Bascobel College, Nashville; Baird College, MO
Bohanan, Joshua	1890	Presbyterian College, Tenn
Bohanan, Levi W.	1888	Batesville, Arkansas
Bond, Henry J	1893-97	Batesville, Arkansas; Commercial College, Ft. Smith, Arkansas
Bowers, Mamie	1893-94	Oak Cliff College, Texas
Bowman, Edward S.	1881	No notation or other information
Burns, E. F.	1891	Batesville, Arkansas
Battiest, Lewis	1888	No notation or other information
Bowers, James	1888	No notation or other information
Beams, Isham		No notation or other information
Beach, Eliza		Mission School, Mississippi
Carney, W. Allen- son of Mosholika		Choctaw Academy, KY; member of Council 1845-46; Died 1875 in Blue County, Choctaw Nation
Calvin, Lewis A.	Bn 1807	Choctaw Academy, Kentucky
Campbell, Charles A	Bn 1818	Choctaw Academy, Kentucky
Cass, Lewis	Bn 1819	Choctaw Academy, KY; Council Member 1871-77; preacher & teacher in 1856
Cass, William	Bn 1819	Choctaw Academy, KY; Member of Council 1855; Member of Constitutional Convention, Skullyville
Camp, Arthur	Bn 1820	Choctaw Academy, Kentucky
Christy, Adam	Bn 1811	Choctaw Academy, KY; Speaker; Chief 1854, 1855 & 1856
Clark, Robert	Bn 1821	Choctaw Academy, Kentucky
Cobb, William- father of L. W. Cobb		Choctaw Academy, KY; member of Council 1873
Coffee, John		Choctaw Academy, Kentucky; taught at one station

Columbus, Lewis	Bn 1816	Choctaw Academy, Kentucky
Columbus, Christ	Bn 1821	Choctaw Academy, Kentucky
Cotton, John R.	Bn 1816	Choctaw Academy, Kentucky
Cornelius, Samuel	Bn 1822	Choctaw Academy, Kentucky
Cornelius, William- son of Capt. Ishtaya	1867	Senator, Red River County; County Judge; District Judge, 2nd District
Cochaunaur, David	Bn 1816	Choctaw Academy, Kentucky
Cochaunaur, Nicholas		Council 1849, Judge 1861 & 1863
Collins, Lyman		Choctaw Academy, Kentucky
Cole, Coleman- son of Robert Cole		Elliot Mission, MS; Council 1855 & 1873; Chief 1874 to 1878; member of Skullyville Convention
Cogswell, Jonathan- father of Daniel Cogwell		Mayhew Mission, MS; Council 1846; Choctaw Name: Iyatochvbbi
Conser, Susie- daughter of Peter Conser	1893-94	Baird College, MO; Central Female College, MO;
Cravatt, Elsie- daughter of Peter Cravatt	1890	Jones Institute, Paris, Texas
Coulte, Anna		Paris, Texas
Choate, Joanna	1890	Central Female College, Mo
Carnell, Wartner J		Notation or other information
Carshall, Jack T.	1894-95	Drury College, Springfield, MO
Cass, O. U.	1895	Drury College, Springfield, MO
Clark, Edwin O.		Central College, Danville, KY; Drury College, MO
Cobb, K. B.	1897	Altus, Ark
Choate, Francis	1890-95	Oswego College, Kansas
Cooley, Edmond	1896	Henry Kendall College, Oklahoma
Clay, Abner- son of Henry Clay	1888	Roanoke College, Virginia; District Chief, 2nd District, 1861
Cooper, Willis	1896	Roanoke College, Virginia; Industrial University, Arkansas
Carney, Annie	1886	Student

Culberson, James	1888	Student
Coons, Claud		Deaf & Mute School, Arkansas
Daniel, Benjamin		Choctaw Academy, KY
Dwight, Johnathan E	Member	Skullyville Convention
Dinsmore, James	Student	Choctaw Academy, KY
Dodge, Lewis	1832	Choctaw Academy, KY
Durant, George- son of A. R. Durant	1832	Choctaw Academy, KY; Circuit Judge 1861; Senator 1878; Supreme Judge 1880
Dwight, Anna	1893-95	Student
Dukes, Loren D.	Student	Batesville, Arkansas
Dukes, Joseph- Son of G. W. Dukes	1891	Batesville, Arkansas; Roanoke College 1892-93
Dyer, Wilburn- son of James Dyer Sr	1891	Roanoke College, Virginia
Dunn, Lena	1886-87	Student
Dwight, Simon T.- father of Ben Dwight	1886-87	Student; Chief 1932; grandfather was Etelheya
Durant, W. A.	1886-87	Student
Durant, Silvester	1863	Trustee, Third District
Dyer, James Sr.- son of Moses Dyer; grandson of Ishtanaki-hacho	1858	Nashville, Tenn
Dana, Daniel		Elliot Mission, Mississippi
Dwight, Edward	Student	Mayhew Mission, Mississippi
Dickinson, Timothy- Choctaw Name: Oklushtubbi	Student	Mission School, Mississippi
Down, Abel- Choctaw Name: Pannshtvbbi	Student	Mission School, Mississippi
Everson, John	Student	Choctaw Academy, KY
Everidge, Edward	Student	Choctaw Academy, KY
Everidge, Sue	1893-94	Baird College, MO; Jones Institute; Oak Cliff College, TX
Everidge, Emma	1890	Jones Institute, Paris, Texas
Everidge, Willie	Student	Paris, Texas

Everidge, Robert	1896	Southwestern Bapt. College, Texas
Everidge, Mary	1887	Student
Fletcher, Benjamin	Student	Choctaw Academy
Fletcher, James	1838-42	District Chief
Franklin, Benjamin	Bn 1813	Choctaw Academy, KY
Franklin, Levi	Student	Choctaw Academy, KY
Franklin, Adam	Bn 1813	Choctaw Academy, KY
Fry, Charles	Bn 1815	Choctaw Academy, KY
Frazier, Timothy	1832	Choctaw Academy, KY
Fransure, T.	Bn 1826	Choctaw Academy, KY
Fransaway, L.	Student	Choctaw Academy, KY
Folsom, Jacob	Student	Choctaw Academy, KY
Folsom, Daniel	Student	Choctaw Academy, KY
Folsom, David Jr.	Student	Choctaw Academy, KY
Folsom, Lewis	Student	Choctaw Academy, KY
Folsom, Peter	Student	Choctaw Academy, KY
Folsom, David	Bn 1791	Died Sept. 27, 1847
Folsom, Henry N	Bn 1815	Choctaw Academy, KY
Folsom, Joseph	Bn 1817	Choctaw Academy, KY
Folsom, Coffee	Bn 1816	Choctaw Academy, KY
Folsom, Joshua	Student	Choctaw Academy, KY
Folsom, Isaac	1841-44	District Chief
Folsom, Amos	Bn 1823	Choctaw Academy, KY
Folsom, E. C.	Bn 1818	Choctaw Academy, KY
Folsom, Joseph R.	Student	Dartmouth College, N.H.

Fisher, Silas D.	1846-50	Third District Chief
Folsom, McKee	Student	Cromwell, Connecticut
Folsom, Israel	Student	Cromwell, Connecticut
Folsom, George	1849	Trustee Neighborhood School
Folsom, John		Attended school in Georgia
Farr, Arthur	1896-97	Bapt. School, Sherman, TX
Folsom, Ida	1897	Jones Institute, Paris, TX
Folsom, Junia	1888	University of Music, Fulton, MO
Freeny, Mary	1897-98	St. Agnes, Antlers, OK
Fisk, Albert	1886-87	Council 1886, 1887 & 1889
Gaines, George G	Bn 1816	Choctaw Academy, KY
Graves, Henry	Student	Choctaw Academy, KY
Gardner, Noel	Student	Choctaw Academy, KY
Garland, Lewis D.	Bn 1818	Choctaw Academy, KY
Gardner, Dona	1887	Jones Institute, Paris, TX
Gardner, Noel	Student	Drury College, Springfield, MO
Gardner, Emma	Student	Drury College, Springfield, MO
Griggs, Lizzie	1892-95	Oxford College, Oxford, Ohio
Gardner, Francis	1895	Baptist Academy
Garland, Sam		Choctaw Academy, KY
Garble, William (Elahonvbbi) Choctaw Name	Student	Mission School, Mississippi
Garland, Joseph	1881	Supreme Judge, First District
Harkins, George W.	Student	Choctaw Academy, KY
Harkins, Willis	Student	Choctaw Academy, KY

Harrison, Zadock	Student	Choctaw Academy, KY
Harrison, William	Bn 1812	Choctaw Academy, KY
Harvey, James	Student	Choctaw Academy, KY
Hall, Joseph R.	1859	National Secretary
Hall, Silas	Student	Choctaw Academy
Harris, Greenwood	Student	Choctaw Academy
Harris, Turner	Student	Choctaw Academy
Hays, Isom	Bn 1824	Choctaw Academy
Harris, C.A.	Bn 1819	Student, Choctaw Academy, KY
Henderson, Thomas	Student	Choctaw Academy, KY
Hays, Marcus	Bn 1826	Student, Choctaw Academy, KY
Holmes, David	Bn 1826	Student, Choctaw Academy, KY
Holson, Stephen	Student	Choctaw Academy, KY -Father of Sam, Noel & Swinney Holson.
Holson, Henry	Student	Choctaw Academy, KY
Holson, Abednego	Bn 1817	Student, Choctaw Academy, KY
Holson, Simeon	Student	Choctaw Academy, KY
Holston, Absolum	Bn 1819	Student, Choctaw Academy, KY
Harkins, Richard	Bn 1813	
Hobert, N	Bn 1816	Student, Choctaw Academy, KY
Hunter, John	Bn 1819	Student, Choctaw Academy, KY
Holly, W. A	Bn 1818	Student, Choctaw Academy, KY
Harris, G	Bn 1816	Student, Choctaw Academy, KY
Hollingshead, William	Student	Mission School, Mississippi
Hinson, Mary	Student	Baird College, Clinton, MO
Howard, Lucy	1897	Jones Institute, Paris, TX

Harris, Lenna	1890	Jones Institute, Paris, TX
Henry, Wilburn H.—son of Amos Henry	1892-97	Drury College, MO
Harrison, Ida	1897	Student, Denison, TX
Hodges, Ozie	1897	Student, Denison, TX
Harkins, Katie	1895	Kidd Key College, TX
Harris, Emily		Paris, TX
Hibdon, Ethel		Paris, TX
Hailey, D. M.		
Hotema, Solomon	1870	Spencer Academy, Roanoke Coll
Hickman, James	1896	Student, Franklin, Tenn
Harrison, Benjamin F		Calvin, OK
Hendrix, Milo	1897	Student, Henry Kendall College
Harrison, Will	1896	Student, Henry Kendall College
Homer, Solomon J	1893	Student, Roanoke College, VA
Hunter, Thomas W.-son of Binahautvbbi	1891-95	Student, Roanoke College, VA
Hodges, John M		
Hebert, Czarina	1886-87	Student
Holson, Mary Jane	1886-87	Student
Hodges, Elizabeth	1886-87	Student
Homer, Joseph	1886-87	Student
Harris, Sallie	1888	Student
Hailey, Lettie	1888	Student
Harrison, Henry C		
Hudson, George		Student, Mayhew Mission, Miss
Hudson, Joel—son of George Hudson		Student, Nashville, Tennessee

Hudson, Napoleon—son of George Hudson		Student, Nashville, Tennessee
Hudson, Wash- father of George Hudson Jr		Captain of Light Horsemen
Hudson, Elsie-daughter of Joel Hudson		Student, Macon, Georgia
Hudson, Peter J.- son of James Hudson	1870-76	Spencer Academy
Hudson, James	1861-73	Member of the Council, Judge
Impson, William	1868-72	Spencer Academy, & Judge
Impson, Josiah	Bn 1825	Choctaw Academy, KY
Ide, Jacob- Choctaw Name: Elahpishtahnvbbi	Student	Mission School, Mississippi
James, Davis D.	Bn 1810	Choctaw Academy, KY
Jenks, William	Student	Mayhew Mission, Mississippi
Jenkins, Jefferson	Bn 1826	Choctaw Academy, KY
Jones, Charles	Bn 1818	Choctaw Academy, KY
Jones, Robert M	1844-48	Council, Choctaw Academy
Jones, Jesse	Bn 1816	Choctaw Academy, Door Keeper of the Choctaw Council-1873
James, John	Bn 1813	Choctaw Academy, KY
Jones, John	Student	Choctaw Academy, KY
Jones, George	Student	Choctaw Academy, KY
Jones, Reason-children: Ellis, Bachariah & Julius	Bn 1824	Choctaw Academy, Council-1860
Jones, Morgan	Bn 1821	Choctaw Academy, KY
Juzan, William	Student	Choctaw Academy, KY
Juzan, Pierre-son of Pierre Juzan	1838-40	District Chief, Third District
James, Charles	Bn 1825	Choctaw Academy, KY
James, George	Bn 1819	Choctaw Academy, KY
James, William	1897	Paris, Texas
Johnson, Wilmon-son of Joe Johnson of Smithville	1887-88	Paris, Texas

Jackson, Florence	1892	Tuskahoma Seminary & Mary Conner College, Paris Texas 1896-97
Jeter, Gertrude	1896-97	Jones Institute & Oak Cliff College
James, Anna	1893-94	Southwestern Bapt. College & Drury College 1895-96
James, Zoda	1896	Central Baptist College
Johnson, Moses	1897	Drury College, MO
Johnson, Willie- son of Wilson N. Jones	1880	Drury College, MO
Jones, Annie- daughter of Wilson N. Jones	1880	Drury College, MO
Jefferson, Winnie	1887	Student
Jefferson, Lewis	1888	Mt Hermon, NH
Jackson, Jacob	1871	Roanke College, Salem, VA
Johnson, Raymond		Son of William Johnson- Iyahaktvbbi
Jenks, William- Choctaw Name: Shukhta	Student	Mission School, Mississippi
King, Peter- son of Miko Mosholetvbbi	Student	Choctaw Academy, KY
King, James- son of Miko Mosholetvbbi	Student	Choctaw Academy, KY
King, Hiram- son of Miko Mosholetvbbi	Student	Choctaw Academy, KY
King, Charley- son of Miko Mosheltvbbi	Student	Choctaw Academy, KY
Kinard, Robert	1861	Judge, First District; Choctaw Academy
King, McKee	1861	Member of Skullyville Convention
Kelly, Ida	1893	Jones Institute, Paris, TX; Cotter College, Nevada 1896-97
Kelly, Elma	1899	Jones Institute, Paris, TX
Krebs, Oscar	1896	Henry Kendall College, Muskogee
Kincaid, Joseph	1836-38	Chief, First District, Choctaw Nation
Krebs, Robert C.	1886-87	Student
Lancaster, Joseph P	Bn 1817	Choctaw Academy, KY

Leonard, Samuel	Bn 1818	Choctaw Academy, KY-died: 1836
Love, Robert	1847	Member of Council
Lewis, Cornelia	1893-94	Baird College, Clinton, MO
Lewis, Dixon W.	1853	Member of Peter Pitchlynn's delegation; died 1856
Leflore, Mary	Student	Baird College, Clinton, MO
Leard, Norman J.	1894	Southwestern Presbyterian College, TN; Henry Kendall College, Muskogee, 1896
Lewis, Nannie (Anna)	1891-93	Oswego College, KS
Locke, V. M. Jr.	Student	Drury College, Springfield, MO
Leflore, Campbell	1886-87	Student
Lawrence, Joshua B.	Student	Mission School, Mississippi
Lewis, Simon		No notations or information
Nail, Morris	Student	Choctaw Academy, KY
Nail, John M	Student	Auditor in 1862; Choctaw Academy, KY
Nail, Joseph	Student	Choctaw Academy; Teacher at Bethabara Mission in 1836
Nail, James	Student	Choctaw Academy, KY
Nail, Joel H.		Died in 1832
Nail, Adam	Bn 1816	Choctaw Academy, KY; Member of Doaksville Convention
Nelson, Brown	Bn 1817	Choctaw Academy, KY
Nail, Benjamin	Bn 1823	Choctaw Academy; Henry Nail married the sister of David Folsom-Jan. 30, 1822. Joel Nail was 25 yrs. Old
Nail, Robert M	Student	Choctaw Academy; Superintendent Schools in 1860
Nail, Ethel	1893-94	Kidd Key College, Sherman, TX
Nail, Katie	1886-87	Student
Nitvkechi	1834-38	Third District Chief
Nash, Sallie	1888	Student

Nelson, Coleman E.	1881	**National Treasurer**
McCan, Wall	Bn 1814	**Choctaw Academy; guardian of Tanitvbbi, son of Ishtanowa**
McClair, John	Bn 1816	**Choctaw Academy, KY**
McGilberry, Harris	Bn 1815	**Choctaw Academy, KY**
McGilbry, James	1836	**Sent home April 1836**
McKinney, Samuel	Bn 1825	**Choctaw Academy, KY**
Morland, B	Bn 1816	**Choctaw Academy, KY**
Moncriff, William	Student	**Choctaw Academy, KY**
McCan, William	Bn 1822	**Choctaw Academy, KY**
Mackey, Alexander	Bn 1827	**Choctaw Academy, KY**
Miller, Daniel	Bn 1818	**Choctaw Academy; Member of Doaksville Convention**
Millard, B	Bn 1817	**Choctaw Academy, KY**
McCan, Lewis	Student	**Choctaw Academy, KY**
McCurtain, Samuel	Student	**Choctaw Academy, KY**
McAfee, Jackson	Student	**Choctaw Academy, KY**
McCurtain, Canady	Student	**Choctaw Academy; Senator-1860 in Sugar Loaf County**
McCurtain, Cornelius	1846-47	**Member of Council; 1850-54 Chief of First District**
McCurtain, Edmond	Bn 1842	**Died: Nov. 11, 1890; no other information**
McCurtain, Camper	Student	**Choctaw Academy, KY**
Mosholetvbbi	1834-36	**Chief of First District**
McKinney, Thompson- mother: Ishtemona; grandmother: Tivkhoma	Bn 1815	**Choctaw Academy; Council member 1847-48 & 1855;**
McKinney, John	1838-42	**Chief of the first District**
McKinney, Thompson		**Son of Judge Mitanvbbi; chief in 1886-87; National Secretary 1880-81**
McKinney, William H.- son of Mitanvbbi	1870	**Spencer Academy**

McCoy, Nelson		**No notations or information**
McCoy, William	1861	**Member of Doaksville Convention; Circuit Judge in 1865**
McIntosh, John	1897	**Drury College, Springfield, MO**
McCurtain, Ida- daughter of Jack & Jane Austin McCurtain	1886	**Baird College, MO; she married Lyman Moore and died in 1931**
McCurtain, Lucinda (Lou)- daughter of Jack and Jane McCurtain	1895	**Baird College, MO; She married Charley Hurd and died: 1930**
McCurtain, David C	Student	**Georgetown University, Wash. D. C.; attorney for the Choctaw Nation**
McCurtain, Cornelius	Student	**Roanoke College, Salem, VA**
McCurtain, Ben	1896	**Henry Kendall College, Muskogee**
McCurtain, Green	Bn 1848	**Henry Kendall College, Muskogee in 1887**
McMurray, Nettie	1897	**Student**
McKinney, Sampson	1892-93	**Lebanon, TN; Austin College 1895-96**
Moore, Lyman	1893	**Boonville, Ark.; Roanoke College, VA**
McEvery, May	Student	**Paris, TX**
McClure, Mary	Student	**St. Agnes, Antlers, OK**
McDaniel, Tom	1896	**Henry Kendall College, Muskogee, IT**
Miller, Robert C.	1886-87	**Student**
Morris, Abbie	1886-87	**Student**
Maytvbbi, Lorinda	1895	**Student**
Moncrief, Katie	1888	**Student**
Miller, Charles William Choctaw name: **Ahnamvtvbbi**	Student	**Mission School, Mississippi;**
McBoyd, Kelso—Choctaw name: **Toshowa**	Student	**Mission School, Mississippi**
Oliphant, Levi Carson – Choctaw Name: **Immakatvbbi**	Student	**Mission School, Mississippi**
Oaks, Daniel	1892-94	**Lamar College, TX; Southwestern Presbyterian College, TN**
Oakes, Lem	1880	**Drury College, MO**
Oakes, Thomas J.	1892	**Drury College, MO**

Oakes, Sue	1897	Oak Cliff College, TX; Jones Institute, TX; Mary Conner, TX- 1895
Page, John	Bn 1820	Choctaw Academy; Member of Council in 1861; Treasurer in 1861
Perry, W. C.	Bn 1825	Choctaw Academy, KY
Perry, Joseph	Student	Choctaw Academy, KY
Perry, Andrew	Student	Choctaw Academy, KY
Perry, James	Student	Choctaw Academy, KY
Perry, Hardy	Student	Choctaw Academy; married Sophia, daughter of Daniel McCurtain
Perry, John	Student	Spencer Academy
Perkins, David	Bn 1817	Choctaw Academy; member of council in 1873
Perkins, George	Bn 1817	Choctaw Academy
Pickens, Solomon		No notations or information
Pitchlynn, William B.	Bn 1824	Choctaw Academy; Auditor 1863; Secretary 1857; Journalist 1873
Pitchlynn, Silas	Student	Choctaw Academy; brother of Peter P. Pitchlynn
Pitchlynn, Ebenezer	Bn 1816	Choctaw Academy, KY
Pitchlynn, John	Bn 1819	Choctaw Academy, KY
Pitchlynn, L. P.	1860	National Secretary
Pitchlynn, Peter Perkins	Bn 1806	University of Nashville; School Trustee; Council member 1861; Chief 1864-66; died: 1881
Pitchlynn, Thomas J.	Bn 1816	Choctaw Academy; Senator in 1855; Commissioner in 1854
Pope, Alexander	Student	Choctaw Academy, KY
Pondexter, George	Student	Choctaw Academy, KY
Pusley, Osborne	Bn 1824	Choctaw Academy, KY
Patterson, James	Student	Mission School, Mississippi; member of council in 1851
Parker, Gabe E.	1896	Henry Kendall College, Muskogee, I.T.
Pitchlynn, Peter	1876-77	Son of Chafvtaya; Council member; Oxford College, OH
Pitchlynn, Alice	Student	Oxford College, Oxford, OH

Pitchlynn, Josie	1896	Baird College, Clinton, MO; Boscobel College, Nashville, TN
Parshall, Lula	Student	Jones Institute, Paris, TX
Pebworth, Emma	Student	Baird College, Clinton, MO
Pickens, Mary	Student	Baird College, Clinton, MO
Pusley, Smallwood	1891-95	Clarksville, Tennessee
Pate, Ella	Student	1888
Radford, Edmond	Student	Choctaw Academy, KY
Riley, James	1860	National Secretary; Member of Choctaw Council in 1861
Riddle, John	Student	Choctaw Academy, KY
Riddle, William	Student	Choctaw Academy, KY
Roebuck, William- son of Zekiel Roebuck	Bn 1822	Choctaw Academy, KY; National Auditor in 1863-65; Member of Council 1860, 1861, 1873
Rosenthall, Ernestine	Student	Jones Institute, Paris, TX
Risner, Carrie	1892-93	Baird College, Clinton, MO; Oxford College, OH
Riddle, Virginia	1886-87	Student
Risner, Caroline	1895	Oxford College, OH
Robb, David	Student	Deaf and Mute School, Orleans, Ill
Stewart, William K	1854-56	Judge; Member of Skullyville Convention; Choctaw Academy, KY
Solomon, Allen	Student	Choctaw Academy, KY
Stewart, Charles J	1860-61	Selected to look after distribution of corn to destitute people; of Red River County
Severs, Ambrose	Bn 1821	Student Choctaw Academy, KY
Smallwood, William	Student	Choctaw Academy, KY; Son of Elijah and Mary (Lefore) Smallwood; Father of Ben Smallwood
Smallwood, Ben	1868-90	Principal Chief; son of William Smallwood
Sherwood, Sophia	Student	Baird College, Clinton, MO
Saxton, Henry	1895	Lamar College, Blossom, TX
Spring, Samuel B	1892-95	Lamar College, Blossom, TX; Southwestern Presbyterian University, TN

Name	Year	School/Notes
Shoney, Wilson	1895	Lamar College, Blossom, TX
Stores, Richard Salter	1822	Mission School, Mississippi
Sexton, Martin	Student	Deaf and Mute School
Spring, Samuel	Student	Mission School, Mississippi
Turnbull, Turner B.	Student	Choctaw Academy, KY; Chief in 1863; Judge in 1853; Council in 1861; Father was John Turnbull
Trahern, George W.	Bn 1815	Choctaw Academy, KY
Trainer, L. B.	Bn 1816	Choctaw Academy, KY
Trahern, James N.	Bn 1810	Choctaw Academy, KY
Taafe, Maud	1897-98	St. Joseph Academy; St. Agnes Academy
Taafe, May	1897	Jones Academy, Paris, TX
Taylor, Ben	1897	Lamar College, TX; Drury College, MO
Taylor, Jones	1896-97	Southwestern Baptist College, Paris, TX; Baptist College, Garland, TX
Thomas, Cleo	1897	Denison, TX
Tennant, Carrie	1892-93	St. Charles MO; Kidd Key College, Garland, TX
Taylor, Ida	1890	Jones Institute, Paris, TX; Central Female College, Lexington, MO
Thompson, Ellis	1893-94	Drury College, MO; Southwestern Presbyterian University, Clarksville, TN
Turnbull, Lizzie	1897-98	St. Agnes Academy, Antlers, OK
Taylor, Hudson	Student	Roanoke College, Salem, VA.
Thompson, Joseph	1886-87	Student
Turnbull, Florence	1896-97	Student
Thompson, James	1863	Supreme Judge, First District
Thompson, Jane	1886-87	Student
Tucker, Hampton	1888	Roanoke College, Salem, VA
Thacker, Robert	1822	Mission School, Mississippi
Tappan, Charles Long- Choctaw name: **Oklushtvbbi**	Student	Mission School, Mississippi

Name	Year/Status	Details
Usray, Josie	Student	Oak Cliff College, TX; Central Female College, MO
Usray, Josephine	Student	Jones Institute, Paris, TX
Vandever, Joseph	Bn 1817	Choctaw Academy, KY
Victor, Wilson	Bn 1825	Choctaw Academy, KY
Victor, Penson	Bn 1827	Choctaw Academy, KY
Vaughn, Loren D.	Student	Drury College, MO; Son of Davis Vaughn; Judge of Wade County, Choctaw Nation
Vinson, Eliza	1886-87	Student
Wales, Biza	1893-94	Jones Institute, Paris, TX
Ward, Bessie	1897	Jones Institute, Paris, TX
Walls, Ida	Student	Baird College, MO
Walker, George	Student	Central College, KY
Walker, Fay	Student	Oxford College, OH
Wooley, Clara	1892-98	St. Agnes, Antlers, OK
Wade, John	Bn 1812	Choctaw Academy, KY; sent home in April 1836
Ward, Silas	Bn 1817	Choctaw Academy, KY
Ward, Nelson	Bn 1819	Choctaw Academy, KY
Wall, David	Student	Choctaw Academy, KY
Wade, Alexander	Bn 1816	Choctaw Academy, KY
Washington, George T	Bn 1816	Choctaw Academy, KY
Washington, George H	Bn 1812	Choctaw Academy, KY
Webster, D. W.	Student	Choctaw Academy, KY
Welch, A. C.	Student	Choctaw Academy, KY
Wilson, Charles	Student	Choctaw Academy, KY
Wilson, David	Student	Choctaw Academy, KY
Wright, Allen Sr.- son of Ishtimahelvbbi	1860-61	Treasurer; member of council-1861; Delegate-1866; Chief- 1866-70; Minister; Superintendent

Name	Date	Notes
Wade, Alfred	Bn 1819	Choctaw Academy; Governor 1857; Council 1861; Skullyville Convention; Treaty 1866
Wade, Jerry	1857-61	Judge; Supreme Judge; Father of Daniel Wade
Wade, Pickens	Student	Choctaw Academy, KY
Ward, William	Student	Choctaw Academy, KY
Wade, Simon	Bn 1817	Choctaw Academy, KY; sent home April 1836
Willis, Simon P.	Bn 1820	Choctaw Academy; Secretary; Doaksville Convention; Council 1877-78; Trustee 1862, 73, 79
Weirs, Andrew	Bn 1817	Choctaw Academy, KY
Wesley, John	Bn 1816	Choctaw Academy, KY
Wright, Benjamin	Student	Choctaw Academy, KY
Wesley, Charles	Student	Choctaw Academy, KY; Brother of Ben Wesley
Worcester, Samuel	Student	Choctaw Academy, KY; died leaving one son Cyrus K. Worcester in 1859
William, Harris	Student	Choctaw Academy, KY
White, Joel	1876-77	Council member; student Choctaw Academy, KY
Woods, Simon	1894	Roanoke College, VA; Batesville, AK; son of Ben Woods; Nephew of Gov. G.W. Dukes
Ward, Timothy	1890-93	Roanoke College, VA
Wilson, Noah	Student	West Norman and Baptist College
Willis, Daisey	Student	Oak Cliff College, TX
William, Silvester	1876-78	Council member
William, Soloman	1870-72	Sheriff
William, Morris	1878-80	Sheriff
Wyett, Jennie	1886-87	Student
Wilson, Sarah	1886-87	Student
William, Alexander	1886-87	Student
Wilson, William P.	1876	Student in Tennessee; Son of Mehataya
William, Aries V.	Student	Mission School, Mississippi

Wright, Dr. E. N.	Student	Union College, Schenectedy, N.Y. died: Jan 1932
Wright, Frank		No notations or information
Wright, Allen Jr.		No notations or information
Wright, James		No notations or information
Wright, Anna		Now Mrs. Ludlow of McAlester, OK
Wright, Carrie		No notations or information
Yotah, Joshua	Student	Drury College, Springfield, MO

Cyrus Byington's list of Choctaw Soldiers, Civil War

This list comes from the Indian Archives
Section X, Cyrus Byington Collection:

1. Simeon Hamilton	1. Wahington Hudson
2. Cyrus Hamilton	2. Johnson—the Big
3. Yakohtambi	3. Hiletvbi
4. Wallace	4. Thompson Hamilton
5. Apototvbi—son of the old Doctor	5. Harris Oklimona's son
6. Hiholbatvbi's non-killed in battle	6. Wallace
7. Isam Going	7. Maya
8. Stephen his nephew	8. Wilson son of Miko Lakna
9. Mambi	9. Jonas Nukhokla
10. Allen	10. Davis Colbert's brother
11. Haya	
12. Apoluma's son	

Hocha's Settlement

Tiliki Bob	John Harrison
Stephen Harrison Tvnvp	William & his brother in law
Halvillechvbi	Iamakentvbi
Imiatvbi	Mishaiontvbi
Tiliki Bob's Nephew	

Men Remaining

1. James Hudson	2. Joshua Dokhannan
3. Moses Dyer	4. Pohvbi
5. Wahumma	6. Ashalintvbi
7. John Buffalo	8. Jordan
9. Filimmetvbi	10. Bill
11. Jackson	12. Oshvn
13. Shiwi	14. Alexander
15. Billy Thomas	16. Nakhacho Humma
17. James Wall's nephew	18. Miashintvbi
19. Captain Baptis	20. David Jones & son
21. Fileta	22. Gilbert Apelatvbi
23. Samuel Apelatvbi	24. Edmund Williams
25. Lyman Collins	26. Rolly Jones an old man
27. Sampson	28. Jefferson
29. Milaicha	30. Simon Jone's brother
31. Jackson Hudson	32. Tanvp-aya
33. Foster	34. Thompson

35. Thomas Howell		36. Peter P. Pitchlynn
37. L. P. Pitchlynn		38. Fileta's son
39. Lewis Hopali		40. Tawantvbi

The other Company

1. Tihlaiatvbi		2. Cornelius
3. Sam Byington's son by **Talowakvbi's wife**		4. Sonny Wakhumma
5. Aivs, Ashalintvbi's nephew & his brother		6. Jo. Burnham
7. Achiahtvbi		8. His Brother
9. Baptist—old man		10. 3 Grand sons
11. Rosamore Christe		12. Peter Howell
13. John Howell		14. Julius Bokhannan
15. Simon Jones		16. H. C. Harris

Soldiers

1. Captain Shoni		2. Jesse Christie
3. Mantvbi		4. J. Taylor
5. Sam Taylor, his son		6. Sam Taylor, his brother
7. Bob Ahekambi		8. Charles Sam
9. Harris Sam		10. James Wall
11. Willys Wall		12. Joseph Iahinlvbi
13. John Sage Favor		14. Lewis—Favor
15. Piabo Baptis		16. Seymour Baptis
17. Lui Tomvtvbi		18. Talowakvbi
19. Impalvmni &		20. Adam, his son
21. Iyapvli		22. Mihateka Jo. Lewis
23. Alston Dyer		24. James Dyer

CHOCTAW ROLL: 1856

We the undersigned, Choctaws, acknowledge the receipts from Douglas H. Cooper, Choctaw Agent of the sum opposite our respective names, being the amounts due us individually in our own right or as representatives of others under whom we claim for the one half of the sum awarded to us by the President of the United States upon sundry reports of Commissions herein after named and invested personages of the Act of the 3rd March 1845 together with the interest on the same up to the 30th June 1852 as per Act of the 21st July 1852:

No. of Certificate	By whom adjudicated	Names of Claimants and Representatives	Amount Paid	Remarks
377A	H & R	Pis-a-hambe Ref. Of Minte Hubbee	$400	April 1, 1856
390C	H & R	Am-be-honal	$100	"
390 A	"	Do Rep. Of Ok-Lee-Homtubbee	$400	"
390 B	"	Do Rep. Of Cuneisb-tunah	$200	"
520 A	"	Hatha-la-hoke Rep. Of Oanubbee	$400	"
520 B	"	Do Rep. Of Tuh-he-kah	$200	"
520 C	"	Do Rep. Of Ah-lo-matabbee	$100	"
353 A	"	Ah-che-ah-tubbee	$400	"
353 B	"	Do Rep. Of Lo-tho-na	$200	"
353 B	"	Oka-in-chuch-mah	$200	"
353 C	"	Chin-alle	$100	"
353 C	"	Ela-nah-tubbee	$100	"
353 C	"	To-no-ho-ka	$100	"
464 A	"	Elah-tah-tubbee Rep. Of Elah-fe-tun-ah	$400	"
464 B	"	Do	$200	"
362 C	"	He-le-honah Rep. Of Ponok-to-chubbee	$100	"
349 A	"	Ela-na-honal Rep. Of Kone-toon-tubbee	$400	"
318 A	"	Ah-na-cho-ka-nah, Yoniab-ho-anb Yoko-tubbee Rep of Now-a-hoka	$400	"
318 B	"	Ah-no-che-honab, Yimab-knonab Kiyo-Kotubbee Rep. Of Hotin-tambe	$200	"

318 B	"	Ah-no-che-honah, Yimah-honab & Hijo-Kotubbee Rep. Of Mocbb-be	$200	"
½ 225 C	H & R	Ho-teah Rep of Mab-no-temah	$ 50	"
½ 225 C	"	Ho-teah	$50	"
383 A	"	I-muk-tab-ubbee & Ille-tubbee Rep. Of Me-she-mah-tubbee	$400	"
383 C	"	Do	$100	"
351 C	"	Eq-le-nubbee	$100	"
351 B	"	Do Rep. Of Pisah-chum-tubbee	$200	"
351 B	"	Do Rep. Of Me-heo-timah	$200	"
297 A	"	Me-hat-te-ubbee, Anook-imah, Loman-tonah & Lammee, Rep of Ah-ish-timah	$400	"
297 B	"	Lamme	$200	"
297 B	"	Anook-imah	$200	"
297 C	"	Lo-man-to-nah	$100	"
297 B	"	Me-hut-to-ubbee, Anookimah, Loman-tonah & Lamme Rep of Belink-attah	$200	"
297 C	"	Me-hut-to-ubbee, Anook-inah, Loman-tonah & Lamme, Rep. Of Ah-to-ko-tubbee	$100	"
385 A	"	She-ne-po-tubbee & Eyah-timah, Reps. Of Ah-tho-me-ho-nah	$400	"
385 C	"	She-ne-po-tubbee	$100	"
385 C	"	Eyah-timah Rep. Of Imah-chiah	$100	"
913 A	"	Si-yimo-hoka Rep. Of Elik-homah	$400	"
913 B	"	Do Rep. Of Ah-onk-timah	$200	"
913 B	"	Do Rep. Of Hik-ah-che	$200	"
343 A	"	Hotich-timah Rep. Of Ah-to-ke-ah-to-nah	$400	"
340 A	"	Elapatimah & Okishtish Rep. Of Couske-koka	$400	"
340 B	"	Do Do Rep. Of Mish-tubbee	$200	"
340 C	"	Elapatimah & Okishtiah Rep. Of Ah-che-tubbee	$100	"
460 B	"	Ah-lo-ka-timah	$200	"
460 A	"	Do Rep. Of Cun-ubbee	$420	"
460 B	"	Do Rep. Of Ah-no-ok-to-cubbee	$ 200	"

458 A	"	Cune-kin-tubbee Rep. Of In-la-cubbee	$400	"
486 B	"	Che-to-kubbee Rep. Of Elah-tah	$200	"
486 B	"	Do Rep. Of Ben	$200	"
486 C	"	Do Rep. Of Tush-ko-lutta	$100	"
487 B	"	La-he-mah Rep. Of Eyah-ah-to-nah	$200	"
281 A	"	Ela-ko-taka	$420	April 4, 1856
281 C	"	Do Rep. Of Eah-ho-chubbee	$105	"
281 C	"	Do Rep. Of Shampo-no-ka	$105	"
276 A	"	Ko-che-ho-ka	$420	"
276 B	"	Do Rep. Of Mah-ah-hiab	$210	"
277 A	"	Ema-le-ho-ka	$420	"
277 C	"	Me-ush-e-mah	$105	"
280 A	"	Unte-cun-a-ubbee Rep. Of Miash-tu-nah	$420	"
280 C	"	Do	$105	"
105 C	C&C	Melissa Rep. Of Jimmy	$100	"
286 A	H & R	Ela-ba-cubbee, Rep. Of Eok-tambee	$400	"
249 C	"	Honah	$100	April 5, 1856
261 A	"	Te-mah, Rep. Of Teah-ke-honab	$420	"
226 A	"	Mo-wah-ho-nah, Rep. Of Ish-teah-honab	$400	"
909 B	"	Do Rep. Of Pe-as-tubbee	$210	"
927 C	W & D	Okis-te-no-nah	$100	"
½ 252 C	H & R	Do (widow) Rep. Of Ela-ya-ka-tubbee	$50	"
796 A	"	Fille-mon-too-nah Rep. Of Ba-che-lah	$400	"
426 B	"	Emah-no-tubbee, Rep. Of Yunetiah	$210	April 7, 1856
888 A	"	Hi-emah, Rep. Of Shatah, Rep. Of Eli-cha-Tubbee	$420	"
903 C	"	Mok-a-tubbee	$100	"
414 B	H & R	Ah-chu-nan-tubbee & Tumbe Rep. Of Timonah	$200	April 7, 1856

469 A	"	Che-a-honah, Rep. Of Ea-ho-ka-tubbee and Rep. Of Isha-hookta	$420	"
435 B	"	Ah-le-hattah	$210	"
851 A	"	Tish-yo-tubbee	$420	"
851 C	"	Ah-no-le-che-nah	$105	"
844 A	"	Mush-shu-le-skak	$420	"
844 C	"	Math-lah-tubbee	$105	"
844 C	"	Ilin-lah-himah	$200	"
405 B	"	Cunes-timah	$200	"
476 A	"	Ho-te-anah	$420	"
476 B	"	Cune-mah-timah & others, Rep. Of Yo-kome-timah	$210	"
476 B	"	Hota-timah	$200	"
939 A	"	Me-ho-nubbee, Rep. Of A-ho-ka	420	"
939 C	"	Do Rep. Of Imah-lubbee	$105	"
933 A	"	Cune-mah-to-mah, Rep. Of Pisambe	$420	"
479 C	"	Pish-ho-timah	$105	"
488 A	"	Hia-la-lo-ka & Pisah-Chubbee, Rep of Cha-ore	$400	"
488 C	"	Pish-le-hubbee, Rep. Is-te-nu-chubbee	$105	"
222 B	M & N	Ah-ho-bah-timah, Rep. Of Ea-han-tubbee	$200	"
483 C	H & R	Onah-tubbee	$105	"
806 A	"	Ah-to-ble-cha	$400	April 16, 1856
806 B	"	Lukey, Rep. Of Cuneah-honah	$210	"
806 B	"	File-ta-honah	$210	"
803 C	"	I-yo-Inan-timah	$100	"
40 C	M & N	Charles	$100	"
824 B	H & R	In-la-teka Landy & Lizzie Ann, Rep. Of Abbe-ho-yo	$200	"
847 B	"	Bucha-ah-honah	$210	"
805 C	"	Leon-von-te-nah-honah	$100	"

841 A	"	Ho-te-akah	$ 400	"
841 C	"	Bessy	$ 100	"
841 C	"	Do Rep. Of Davis	$ 100	"
820 A	H & R	Ah-chi-ah	$420	Ap. 16, 1856
188 A	C & C	Cun-ne-tambee Rep. Of Kotah	$420	"
188 C	"	Cun-ne-tambe	$105	"
79 B	"	Illah-haynto-nah- or Tonah	$200	"
79 A	"	Do Rep. Of Atahah	$400	"
79 B	"	Do Rep. Of Mockan-tubbee	$200	"
143 A	"	Ah-to-sho-ubbee, Rep. Of Lomah	$420	Ap 17, 1856
143 B	"	Do	$ 210	"
142 B	"	Eah-tubbee	$ 210	"
252 A	H & R	Look-a-la-tubbee	$400	"
½ 252 C	"	Do Rep. Of Ela-yo-ka-tubbee	$50	"
142 C	C & C	Ema-no-wa-ubbee, Rep. Of Ah-pah-la-bonah	$100	"
153 B	"	Olu-bbee-to-nah	$200	"
5 A	"	Hatona Rep. Of Pom-fillah	$ 420	"
5 C	"	Do Rep. Of Meah-to-ubbee	$ 105	"
98 A	"	Jesse Rep. Of Ah-fo-to-tubbee	$400	"
98 B	"	Ah-chah-fah-tomah, Rep. Of Jesse	$200	"
113 B	M & N	Im-mis-to-nah	$210	"
111 B	C & C	Tith-lo-ho-nah	$210	"
111 B	C & C	Putte	$ 200	"
111 C	"	Jamah	$ 100	"
951 A	W & D	Nocke-ne-hiah, Rep. Of Ola-tubbee & of Ish-to-me-hah-tubbee	$ 420	Apr 19, 1856
307 A	H & R	Nocke-ne-hiah, Rep. Of Imah-tho-ya	$400	"
307 B	"	Do Rep. Of Pots-le-chubbee	$ 200	"

307 B	"	Do Rep. Of Elah-u-kah	$ 200	"
676 A	"	Pish-te-she-mah, Rep. Of Ma-hambee	$400	"
676 C	"	Do, Rep. Of Ish-te-mah	$ 100	"
676 C	"	Do, Rep. Of Temo-nah	$ 100	"
676 C	"	Pish-te-she-mah	$ 100	"
501 A	"	Tamoah Rep. Of In-ta-hubbee	$420	"
501 C	"	Do, Rep. Of hna-timah	$ 105	"
222 B	M & N	Ea-chubbee	$ 200	"
608 B	H & R	Pisah-honah, Rep. Of Hi-yok-ah	$ 200	"
156 A	C & C	Illa-mowa, Rep. Of Elah-umbbee	$ 400	"
710 C	H & R	Potah	$ 100	"
550 A	"	Mulla-le-chubbee	$ 400	"
710 A	"	Potah, Rep. Of Ela-hoyo	$ 400	"
½ 733 A	"	Ela-fulle-tubbee, Rep. Of Nok-ho-ma-ho-yo	$210	"
½ 733 B	"	Do, Rep. Of Chuffa-tiah & Ah-chuk-ma-hoka	$ 210	"
710 B	"	Hia-la	$200	"
710 B	"	Im-mille	$ 200	"
550 B	"	Kun-nal-le-tubbee	$ 200	"
550 B	"	Do, Rep. Of Ok-lio-Oka	$ 200	"
550 C	"	Do, Rep. Of Phile-ah-hoyo	$ 100	"
855 A	"	Hiok-lah, Rep. Of Lath-leyo	$ 400	"
220 A	"	Nowah-ho-ka	$ 400	"
220 B	"	Imah-le-honah	$ 200	"
344 B	"	Pisah-ti-mah	$ 200	"
342 A	"	Ish-im-ah-hoka	$ 400	"
342 B	"	Wilson, Rep. Of Ish-te-mi-onah	$ 200	"
342 C	"	Wilson, Rep. Of Cuna-Oua-honah	$ 100	"

392 C	"	Onah-te-mah	$ 100	"
311 A	"	Ke-kah-te-nah, Rep. Of Anun-tubbee	$ 400	"
311 B	"	Do	$ 200	"
311 B	"	Do, Rep. Of Amah	$ 200	"
362 A	"	Hick-a-timah, Rep. Of Me-hah-tah-tah	$ 400	"
459 A	"	Cunoon-tambe & Yohab-to-nah, Rep. Of Temalah	$ 400	"
255 A	"	Okla-me-ashab	$100	"
255 C	"	Hotah-ah-tubbee	$200	"
255 B	"	Imah-hoka, Rep. Of Cunun-tah-mah	$ 200	"
255 B	"	Do, Rep. Of Cunun-tuh-bee	$ 210	"
73 B	H & R	Pisah-ti-mah, Rep. Of Meshum-tah-tubbee	$ 210	Apr. 24, 1856
889 A	"	Hote-Chubbee, Rep. Of Ish-to-mah	$ 400	May 5, 1856
889 B	"	Do Rep. Of Kah-no-me-hemah	$ 200	"
889 B	"	Do. Rep. Of Hie-ha-tesho	$ 200	"
889 C	"	Do. Rep. Of Ish-tah-Pok-nah	$ 100	"
691 B	"	Oatha-che, Rep. Of Mea-sho-ste Mah-Imah-ho-nah, Rep. Of Emah-tambe	$210	"
966 A	W & D	Hos-too-nah	$ 400	"
966 B	"	Do, Rep. Of Fhicte-ma-emah-tubbee	$ 200	"
966 B	"	Do, Rep. Of Elah-I-ke-bah	$ 200	"
966 C	"	Do, Rep. Of Chakio-tubbee	$ 100	"
601 A	H & R	Pish-no-ubbee, Rep. Of Talo-moon-tubbee	$ 400	"
601 C	"	Do, Rep. Of Ok-la-hah	$ 100	"
613 A	"	Lak-nache-honah	$ 400	"
613 B	"	Ok-le-mah-cheah-honah	$ 200	"
613 C	"	Weah-honah	$ 200	"
613 C	"	Ok-le-mah-che-ah-honah & Wea-honah Rep. Of Tah-ne-honah	$100	"
704 B	"	Imish-tiah Rep. Of Lapom-ah-hah	$200	"

704 B	"	Do " " Hisler	$200	"
704 C	"	" " "	$100	"
549 A	"	Pish-no-ubbee Rep. Of Piyah-hoocta	$400	"
611 C	"	Wallace	$100	May 6, 1856
611 A	"	Do ½ Rep. Of Ebab-kah-lubbee	$200	"
514 B	"	Ah-chuck-ah-mah	$200	"
218 B	M&V	Ean-puka-nubbee	$200	"
791 C	H&R	Chon-pah-to-nah	$105	"
65 B	WD	Elo-na-chubbee	$200	May 20, 1856
65 C	WD	Eme-la-hona	$100	"
40 C	C&G	A-low-a-honah	$100	"
199 A	C & C	Chitto-tah	$420	May 20, 1856
192 A	C & C	Loma-taka	$400	"
192 C	C & C	Lab-a-che	$100	"
124 C	W & D	Salla	$100	"
162 A	C & C	Slowe Temah & Im-mock-a-honah Rep. Of Ash-te-mah-ka	$400	"
162 B	C & C	Im-mock-a-honah	$200	"
162 C	C & C	Elowe-temah & Im-mock-a-honab Rep. Of Cun-noon-tah-cubbee	$100	"
18 C	"	Eah-le-honah	$100	"
42 C	W D	Liza Ann	$100	"
7 B	C & C	Jamab	$200	"
7 B	C & C	Do Rep. Of Me-his-tubbee	$200	"
94 C	"	Ah-lab-hoto-nah	$100	"
22 C	"	Hi-ala	$100	"
406 C	W D	Ala-te-nah	$100	"
127 C	C & C	Betsy Cobb Rep. Of Celia	$105	"
93 C	W D	Lilliam Rep. Of Dennis	$100	"

27 C	M & T	An-ain-tubbee, Rep. Of Alan-an-tubbee	$100	"
141 A	C & C	Im-mah-hoba, Rep. Of Co-chubbee	$420	"
141 B	C & C	Do Rep. Of Teni-yah-tubbee	$210	"
141 C	"	Do Rep. Of Ah-min-tubbee	$105	"
135 B	W D	Im-ah-honah Rep. Of Ah-ho-nah	$200	"
300 A	H & R	Mohah Rep. Of Coah-ho-mah	$400	"
406 B	"	Sho-ti-mah Rep. Of Me-ayo-to-nah	$210	"
169 B	C & C	Lee-la-honab & Una-ha-timab, Rep. Of Ah-be-bah-tab	$200	"
220 B	M & W	Ah-pe-la-honab, Rep. Of Im-milohonab	$200	May 20, 1856
189 B	"	Il-la-mo-to-nah	$200	"
189 A	"	Do Rep. Of Eab-sha-tubbee	$400	"
641 B	H & R	Illiokso, Rep. Of Heith-lah-honab	$200	"
669 A	H & R	Hoto-kubbee, Rep. Of Hobe-ti-yah	$400	May 29, 1856
669 C	"	Do	$100	"
669 C	"	Do " " Yoko-temah	$100	"
209 C	W D	Een-ta-hoka	$100	"
186 B	"	Me-ha-to-na	$200	"
186 C	"	Apela-honah, Rep of Is-tubbee	$100	"
186 C	"	Me-ha-to-nah & Apela-honh, Rep. Of Ona-hema	$100	"
812 A	H & R	Sally, Rep of Take-uniye	$400	"
862 B	"	Do	$200	"
862 C	"	Do " Polly	$100	"
614 C	"	Chuffa-to-no-wah	$100	"
614 A	"	Do Rep. Of Eya-tu-nah	$400	"
227 B	M & N	Anolehoyo, Rep of Cunnea-tubbee	$200	"
227 B	"	Do Rep. Of Temaka	$200	"
735 B	H & R	Iokle, Rep of To-bulle	$200	"

735 B	"	Do Rep. Of Me-haw	$200	"
28 C	W D	Ish-tiope , Rep. Of Shampi-omah	$100	"
759 B	H & R	I-te-him-tubbee, Rep. Of Ash-kama	$210	"
577 B	"	Pah-ke-ti-mah, Rep. Of Is-mah-to-nah	$210	"
718 B	"	Meashia, Rep. Of Temah	$200	"
574 A	"	Pisah-chish-e-mah, Rep. Of Me-skambe	$400	"
577 B	"	Elie-katubbee, Rep. Of Kah-nu-mah-hamah	$200	"
541 B	"	Ish-li-yah	$200	"
541 B	"	Do & Cumes-tubbee, Rep. Of Me-cambe	$200	"
541 B	"	Ish-li-yah & Cumes-tubbee, Rep. Of Tooka-chubbee	$200	"
541 C	"	Do Do Rep. Of Cha-wabbe	$ 100	"
541 C	"	Do Do Rep. Of Tick-ba-oonah	$100	"
186 C	W D	Tuk-a-lubbee	$100	"
186 C	"	Piso-tubbee	$100	"
400 B	H & R	Ho-teaka	$200	"
400 C	"	Kanoon-ubbee	$100	"
399 A	"	Oon-tah-yubbee, Rep. Of Ulth-la-honab	$400	May, 1856
399 B	"	Do Rep. Of Ho-chubbee	$200	"
630 B	"	Lomoah-honab, Rep. Of Lame-wah-honah	$200	"
486 B	"	Pash-chubbee & others, Rep. Of Hopokonah	$210	"

We certify that we were present during the payment of the foregoing amounts: the sums set opposite their respective names were paid to the several Indians in specific and that their signature or mark were affixed in the presence: **E. S. Mitchell**, **N. B. Breedlove** and **A. L. Morris**

We the undersigned chiefs and principal men of our respective parties do hereby acknowledge the corrections of the foregoing receipts and certified that the sums to which the several claimants are entitled for Principal and Interest on awards under the 14th Article of the treaty of 1830 were paid to them in an presence in accordance with the act of Congress of the 21st of June 1852.

In the presence of
John Page, US Interpreter
For the Choctaws:
Panshiah-to-nah-mah   Yosho-yo-tubbee
Folook-ache   Mullo-le-chubbee
Abbe-tuttah   Ben-le-Florol
Tombbee   Mea-Shico

Ela-la-cubbee
Nock-ne-hiab
Ho-to-chubbee
Chil-le-tah
Yim-me-tubbee
In-co-chubbee
Hozubbee or **Jim Porter**

I certify, to honor, that I have actually paid the several sum in the foregoing Rolls as therein set forth the commencing April 1st and ending May 24th 1856. Signed: **Douglas H. Cooper,** US Indian Agent

Rhoda Pitchlynn Howell's Bible Records:

The following bible records belonged to a prominent Choctaw Indian citizen of Indian Territory. Rhoda Pitchlynn, who married Calvin H. Howell, was a descendant of the famous Pitchlynn family of the Choctaw Nation.

Name in Bible Record	Birthdate	Death
John Pitchlynn	June 11, 1764	May 20, 1835
Sophia F. Pitchlynn	Dec. 27, 1786	
Peter Pitchlynn	Jan 20, 1806	
Charley Pitchlynn	Nov. 14, 1807	
Silas Pitchlynn	Dec. 17, 1809	
Mary Pitchlynn	Oct. 13, 1811	
Rhoda Pitchlynn	Jan. 31, 1814	
Thomas J. Pitchlynn	Jan. 15, 1816	
A. C. Pitchlynn	Jan 14, 1818	
Elizabeth C. Pitchlynn	April 3, 1820	
Sariah Pitchlynn	July 6, 1824	
Calvin H. Howell	May 28, 1799	Oct. 1, 1865
William F. Howell	Aug. 15, 1829	
Isabell Howell	Sept. 10, 1830	Aug. 15, 1867
Arabell Howell	Feb. 22, 1932	Nov. 9, 1878
Margaret Howell	Oct. 13, 1834	Oct. 13, 1895
Joseph Howell	March 22, 1836	
John T. Howell	Feb. 26, 1839	Feb. 15, 1900
Peter P. Howell	Dec. 15, 1839	Feb. 15, 1865
Mary C. Howell	March 4, 1841	Dec. 16, 1910
Calvin C. B. Howell	March 4, 1843	Dec. 16, 1910
Elmer Ed. Howell	Sept. 22, 1844	
Elizabeth R. Howell	June 28, 1846	Oct. 1878
Thomas P. Howell	Aug. 11, 1849	July 16, 1943

| Ellen Howell | July 28, 1851 | |
| Fannie S. Howell | May 26, 1856 | Jan 24, 1908 |

The note at the end of the Bible record stated that John Pitchlynn was a white man who married a ½ breed Indian woman. John Pitchlynn died in 1835.

INDEX

A

- **Abbe-ho-yo** 31
- Abbe-tuttah 37
- Achela 2
- Adam 27
- Adams Missie 7
- Adams Mitchell C 7
- Adams, John 7
- **Ah-be-bah-tab** 36
- **Ah-chah-fah-tomah** 32
- **Ah-che-ah-tubbee** 28
- **Ah-che-tubbee** 29
- **Ah-chi-ah** 32
- **Ah-chuck-ah-mah** 35
- **Ah-chuk-ma-hoka** 33
- **Ah-chu-nan-tubbee** 30
- **Ah-fo-to-tubbee** 32
- **Ah-ho-bah-timah** 31
- **Ah-ho-nah** 36
- **Ah-ish-timah** 29
- **Ah-lab-hoto-nah** 35
- Ahlasih 1
- **Ah-le-hattah** 31
- **Ah-lo-ka-timah** 29
- **Ah-lo-matabbee** 28
- Ahl-sih *3*
- **Ah-min-tubbee** 36
- **Ah-na-cho-ka-nah** 28
- Ah-ni-nie 3
- **Ah-no-che-honab,** 28
- **Ah-no-che-honah** 29
- **Ah-no-le-che-nah** 31
- **Ah-no-ok-to-cubbee** 29
- **A-ho-ka** 31
- **Ah-onk-timah** 29
- **Ah-pah-la-bonah** 32
- **Ah-pe-la-honab** 36
- **Ah-tho-me-ho-nah** 29
- **Ah-to-ble-cha** 31
- **Ah-to-ke-ah-to-nah** 29
- **Ah-to-ko-tubbee** 29
- **Ah-to-sho-ubbee** 32
- Ainsworth James 7
- Ainsworth Jessie 7
- Ainsworth Napoleon B 7
- Ainsworth Thomas D 7
- **Alan-an-tubbee** 36
- **Ala-te-nah** 35
- Alexander 26
- Allen 25
- Allen, Samuel 7
- **A-low-a-honah** 35
- **Amah** 34
- **Am-be-honal** 28
- **An-ain-tubbee** 36
- A-na-soo-yah
  - Mix Water 1
- **Anolehoyo** 36
- **Anook-imah** 29
- **Anun-tubbee** 34
- **Apela-honah** 36
- **Apela-honh** 36
- Apelatvbi 26
- Apoluma's 25
- Apototvbi 25
- Appliton Jesse 7
- Arka-loo-ka   John *4*
- Ashalintvbi 26
- **Ash-kama** 37
- **Ash-te-mah-ka** 35
- Atahah 32
- Auston, John 7

B

- **Ba-che-lah** 30
- Barbour James 7
- Battiest Fransaway 7
- Battiest Lewis *8*
- Baxter Richard 7
- Beach Eliza *8*
- Beams Isham *8*
- **Belink-attah** 29
- Belvin Watson J *8*
- **Ben** 30
- Benjamin *5*
- **Bessy** 32
- Bill 26
- Billy Thomas 26
- Birch Sampson 7
- Black James D 7
- Bohanan Joshua *8*
- Bohanan Levi W *8*
- Bond Henry J *8*
- Bowers James *8*
- Bowers Mamie *8*
- Bowman Edward S *8*
- Brainard Millard 7
- Brainard Thomas 7
- Brandan J. C. 7
- Breashears Charley 7
- Brewer Elijah 7
- Brewer James 7
- Brown Myrtle *8*
- Brown Silas 7
- Bryant William 7
- **Bucha-ah-honah** 31
- Buckhold August **8**
- Buffalo 26
- **bulle** 36
- Burnham 27
- Burns E. F. *8*
- Burris Gabriel 7
- Byington Thomas H *8*
- Byington, Sam 27
- Byinton Jerrymiah *8*

C

Name	Page
Calvin Lewis A.	8
Camp, Arthur	8
Campbell Charles A.	8
Captain Baptis	26
Carnell, Wartner J.	9
Carney W Allen	8
Carney, Annie	9
Carshall, Jack T	9
Cass Lewis	8
Cass, O. U	9
Cass, William	8
Celia	35
Chakio-tubbee	34
Cha-ore	31
Charles	31
Charles Sam	27
Charley	3, 5
Cha-wabbe	37
Che-a-honah	31
Che-ah-sa-hi	3
Che-to-kubbee	30
Chil-le-tah	38
Chin-alle	28
Chitto-tah	35
Choate, Francis	9
Choate, Joanna	9
Chon-pah-to-nah	35
Christy, Adam	8
Chuffa-tiah	33
Chuffa-to-no-wah	36
Clark, Edwin O.	9
Clark, Robert	8
Clay, Abner	9
Coah-ho-mah	36
Cobb Betsy	35
Cobb, K. B.	9
Cobb, William	8
Cochaunaur, David	9
Cochaunaur, Nicholas	9
Co-chubbee	36
Coffee, John	8
Cogswell, Jonathan	9
Cole, Coleman	9
Collins, Lyman	9
Columbus, Christ	9
Columbus, Lewis	9
Conser, Susie	9
Cooley, Edmond	9
Coons, Claud	10
Cooper, Douglas H	38
Cooper, Willis	9
Cornelius	27
Cornelius, Samuel	9
Cornelius, William	9
Cotton, John R.	9
Coulte, Anna	9
Couske-koka	29
Co-wa-la-skih	4
Cravatt, Elsie	9
Culberson, James	10
Cul-stih-yih	3
Cumes-tubbee	37
Cuna-Oua-honah	33
Cuneah-honah	31
Cune-kin-tubbee	30
Cune-mah-timah	31
Cune-mah-to-mah	31
Cunes-timah	31
Cunnea-tubbee	36
Cun-ne-tambe	32
Cun-ne-tambee	32
Cun-noon-tah-cubbee	35
Cunoon-tambe	34
Cun-ubbee	29
Cunun-tah-mah	34
Cunun-tuh-bee	34
Cyrus Byington	25

D

Name	Page
Dah-hah & Cha-wa-louge	1
Dana, Daniel	10
Daniel, Benjamin	10
David Jones	26
Davis	32
Davis Betsy	
Thomas, Monroe, Neppa, George	1
Davis Colbert's	25
Dennis	35
Dickinson, Timothy	10
Dilly	5
Dinsmore, James	10
Dodge, Lewis	10
Dokhannan	26
Down, Abel	10
Dukes, Joseph	10
Dukes, Loren D.	10
Dunn, Lena	10
Durant, George	10
Durant, Silvester	10
Durant, W. A.	10
Dwight, Anna	10
Dwight, Edward	10
Dwight, Johnahan E.	10
Dwight, Simon T	10
Dyer, James	27
Dyer, James Sr	10
Dyer, Wilburn	10

E

Name	Page
Eab-sha-tubbee	36
Ea-chubbee	33
Ea-han-tubbee	31
Eah-ho-chubbee	30
Eah-le-honah	35
Ea-ho-ka-tubbee	31
Eah-tubbee	32
Ean-puka-nubbee	35
Eastern Cherokee	
Annuity	1
Ebab-kah-lubbee	35
Edmund Williams	26

Een-ta-hoka	36
Ela-ba-cubbee	30
Ela-fulle-tubbee	33
Elah-fe-tun-ah	28
Elah-I-ke-bah	34
Ela-hoyo	33
Elah-tah	30
Elah-tah-tubbee	28
Elah-u-kah	33
Elah-umbbee	33
Ela-ko-taka	30
Ela-la-cubbee	38
Ela-na-honal	28
Ela-nah-tubbee	28
Elapatimah	29
Ela-ya-ka-tubbee	30
Ela-yo-ka-tubbee	32
Eli-cha-Tubbee	30
Elie-katubbee	37
Elik-homah	29
Ellan-a-you-na-cah	*4*
Ellek	*3*
Elo-na-chubbee	35
Elowe-temah	35
Emah-no-tubbee	30
Emah-tambe	34
Ema-le-ho-ka	30
Ema-no-wa-ubbee	32
Eme-la-hona	35
Eok-tambee	30
Eq-le-nubbee	29
Everidge, Edward	*10*
Everidge, Emma	*10*
Everidge, Mary	*11*
Everidge, Robert	*11*
Everidge, Sue	*10*
Everidge, Willie	*10*
Everson, John	*10*
Eyah-ah-to-nah	30
Eyah-timah	29
Eya-tu-nah	36
Ezekiel	3

F

Farr, Arthur	*12*
Fhicte-ma-emah-tubbee	34
Fileta	26
Fileta's	27
File-ta-honah	31
Filimmetvbi	26
Fille-mon-too-nah	30
Fisher, Silas D	*12*
Fisk, Albert	*12*
Fletcher, Benjamin	*11*
Fletcher, James	*11*
Flower	1
Folook-ache	37
Folsom, Amos	*11*
Folsom, Coffee	*11*
Folsom, Daniel	*11*
Folsom, David	*11*
Folsom, David Jr	*11*
Folsom, E C	*11*
Folsom, George	*12*
Folsom, Henry N	*11*
Folsom, Ida	*12*
Folsom, Isaac	*11*
Folsom, Israel	*12*
Folsom, Jacob	*11*
Folsom, John	*12*
Folsom, Joseph	*11*
Folsom, Joseph R	*11*
Folsom, Joshua	*11*
Folsom, Junia	*12*
Folsom, Lewis	*11*
Folsom, McKee	*12*
Folsom, Peter	*11*
Foster	26
Franklin, Adam	*11*
Franklin, Benjamin	*11*
Franklin, Levi	*11*
Fransaway, L	*11*
Fransure, T	*11*
Frazier, Timothy	*11*
Freeny, Mary	*12*
Fry, Charles	*11*

G

Gaines, George G	*12*
Garble, William	*12*
Gardner, Dona	*12*
Gardner, Emma	*12*
Gardner, Francis	*12*
Gardner, Noel	*12*
Garland, Joseph	*12*
Garland, Lewis D	*12*
Garland, Sam	*12*
Graves, Henry	*12*
Griggs, Lizzie	*12*

H

Hailey, D. M.	*14*
Hailey, Lettie	14
Hall Joseph R	*13*
Hall, Silas	*13*
Halvillechvbi	26
Hamilton	25
Hamilton, Cyrus	25
Harkins, George W	*12*
Harkins, Katie	*14*
Harkins, Richard	*13*
Harkins, Willis	*12*
Harris, C. A.	*13*
Harris, Emily	*14*
Harris, G.	*13*
Harris, Greenwood	*13*
Harris, H. C.	27
Harris, Lenna	*14*
Harris, Sallie	*14*
Harris, Turner	*13*
Harrison, Benjamin F	*14*
Harrison, Henry C	*14*

Name	Page
Harrison, Ida	*14*
Harrison, Will	14
Harrison, William	*13*
Harrison, Zadock	*13*
Harvey, James	*13*
Hatona	32
Haya	25
Hays, Isom	*13*
Hays, Marcus	*13*
Hebert, Czarina	*14*
Heith-lah-honab	36
He-le-honah	28
Henderson, Thomas	*13*
Hendrix, Milo	14
Henry, Wilburn H	*14*
Henson M	*4*
Henson Sarah	1
Henson William	*5*
Hi-ala	35
Hia-la	33
Hia-la-lo-ka	31
Hibdon, Ethel	*14*
Hick-a-timah	34
Hickman, James	*14*
Hie-ha-tesho	34
Hi-emah	30
Hiholbatvbi's	25
Hijo-Kotubbee	29
Hik-ah-che	29
Hiletvbi	25
Hinson, Mary	*13*
Hiok-lah	33
Hisler	35
Hi-yok-ah	33
hna-timah	33
Hobe-ti-yah	36
Ho-chubbee	37
Hodges, Elizabeth	14
Hodges, John M	14
Hodges, Ozie	14
Holbert, N	*13*
Hollingshead, William	*13*
Holly, W. A.	*13*
Holmes, David	*13*
Holson, Abednego	*13*
Holson, Henry	*13*
Holson, Mary Jane	14
Holson, Simeon	*13*
Holson, Stephen	*13*
Holston, Absolum	*13*
Homer, Joseph	14
Homer, Solomon J	14
Honah	30
Hopokonah	37
Hos-too-nah	34
Hotah-ah-tubbee	34
Hota-timah	31
Ho-teah	29
Ho-teaka	37
Ho-te-akah	32
Ho-te-anah	31
Hote-Chubbee	34
Hotema, Solomon	*14*
Hotich-timah	29
Hotin-tambe	28
Ho-to-chubbee	38
Hoto-kubbee	36
How-a-qrua	1
Howard, Lucy	*13*
Howell, Arabell	39
Howell, Calvin C. B.	39
Howell, Calvin H	39
Howell, Elizabeth R	39
Howell, Ellen	40
Howell, Elmer Ed	39
Howell, Fannie S	40
Howell, Isabell	39
Howell, John T	39
Howell, Joseph	39
Howell, Margaret	39
Howell, Mary C	39
Howell, Peter	27
Howell, Peter P	39
Howell, Thomas P	39
Howell, William F	39
Hozubbee	38
Hudson, Elsie dauther of Joel Hudson	15
Hudson, George	14
Hudson, James	15
Hudson, Joel	*See* son of George Hudson
Hudson, Napoleon	*See* son of George Hudson
Hudson, Peter J	*See* son of James Hudson
Hudson, Wash father of George Hudson Jr.	15
Hunter, John	*13*
Hunter, Thomas W.-	14

I

Name	Page
Iahinlvbi	27
Iamakentvbi	26
Ide, Jacob	*See* Elahpishtahnvbbi
Ilin-lah-himah	31
Illah-haynto-nah	32
Il-la-mo-to-nah	36
Illa-mowa	33
Ille-tubbee	29
Illiokso	36
Imah-chiah	29
Imah-hoka	34
Im-ah-honah	36
Imah-le-honah	33
Imah-lubbee	31
Imah-tho-ya	32
Imiatvbi	26
Imish-tiah	34
Im-mah-hoba	36
Im-mille	33
Im-milohonab	36
Im-mis-to-nah	32
Im-mock-a-honab	35
Im-mock-a-honah	35

Impson, Josiah	15
Impson, William	15
I-muk-tab-ubbee	29
In-co-chubbee	38
In-la-cubbee	30
In-la-teka Landy	31
In-ta-hubbee	33
Iokle	36
Isam Going	25
Isha-hookta	31
Ish-im-ah-hoka	33
Ish-li-yah	37
Ish-tah-Pok-nah	34
Ish-teah-honab	30
Ish-te-mah	33
Ish-te-mi-onah	33
Ish-tiope	37
Ish-to-mah	34
Ish-to-me-hah-tubbee	32
Is-mah-to-nah	37
Is-te-nu-chubbee	31
Is-tubbee	36
I-te-him-tubbee	37
I-yo-Inan-timah	31

J

Jack	5
Jackson	26
Jackson Hudson	26
Jackson, Florence	16
Jackson, Jacob	16
Jamab	35
Jamah	32
James Hudson	26
James Wall's	26
James, Anna	16
James, Charles	15
James, Davis D	15
James, George	15
James, John	15
James, William	15
James, Zoda	16
Jefferson	26
Jefferson, Lewis	16
Jefferson, Winnie	16
Jek-hin-nih Wilson	2
Jenkins, Jefferson	15
Jenks, William	15. *See* Shukhta
Jesse	32
Jesse Christie	27
Jeter, Gertrude	16
Jimmy	30
John	5
John Harrison	26
Johnson	25
Johnson, Moses	16
Johnson, Raymond	16
Johnson, Willie	*See* Wilson N Jones
Johnson, Wilmon	*See* Joe Johnson
Jones John B US Indian Agent	1
Jones, Annie	*See* Wilson N Jones
Jones, Charles	15
Jones, George	15
Jones, Jesse	15
Jones, John	15
Jones, Morgan	15
Jones, Reason	*See* Ellis, Bachariah & Julius
Jones, Robert M	15
Jordan	26
Josiah	1
Judah	5
Julius Bokhannan	27
Ju-na-lus-kih	2
Juzan, Pierre	*See* son of Pierre Juzan
Juzan, William	15

K

Kah-no-me-hemah	34
Kah-nu-mah-hamah	37
Kanoon-ubbee	37
Ka-ta-ih	1
Ke-kah-te-nah	34
Kelly, Elma	16
Kelly, Ida	16
Kinard, Robert	16
Kincaid, Joseph	16
King, Charley	*See* Miko Mosheltvbbi
King, Hiram	*See* Miko Mosholetvbbi
King, James	*See* Miko-Mosholetvbbi
King, McKee	16
King, Peter	*See* Miko Mosholetvbbi
Kinn	5
Ko-che-ho-ka	30
Kone-toon-tubbee	28
Kotah	32
Krebs, Oscar	16
Krebs, Robert C	16
Kun-nal-le-tubbee	33

L

L. P. Pitchlynn	27
Lab-a-che	35
La-he-mah	30
Lak-nache-honah	34
Lame-wah-honah	37
Lamme	29
Lancaster, Joseph P	16
Lapom-ah-hah	34
Lath-leyo	33
Lawrence, Joshua B	17
Leard, Norman J	17
Lee-la-honab	36
Leflore, Campbell	17
Leflore, Mary	17
Leonard, Samuel	17
Leon-von-te-nah-honah	31
Lewis Hopali	27
Lewis, Cornelia	17
Lewis, Dixon W	17
Lewis, Nannie (Anna)	17
Lewis, Simon	17

Lewis—Favor	27
Lilliam	35
Linda	3
Liza Ann	35
Lizzie Ann	31
Locke, V. M. Jr.	17
Locust Joe	3
Lomah	32
Lo-man-to-nah	29
Loma-taka	35
Lomoah-honab	37
Look-a-la-tubbee	32
Lo-tho-na	28
Love, Robert	17
Lucy	3
Lukey	31
Lydia	3
Lyman Collins	26

M

Mab-no-temah	29
Mackey, Alexander	18
Mah-ah-hiab	30
Ma-hambee	33
Mah-Imah-ho-nah	34
Mambi	25
Mary	5
Math-lah-tubbee	31
Maya	25
Maytvbbi, Lorinda	19
McAfee, Jackson	18
McBoyd, Kelso	*See* Toshowa
McCan, Lewis	18
McCan, Wall	18
McCan, William	18
McClair, John	18
McClure, Mary	19
McCoy, Nelson	19
McCoy, William	19
McCurtain, Ben	19
McCurtain, Camper	18
McCurtain, Canady	18
McCurtain, Cornelius	18, 19
McCurtain, David C	19
McCurtain, Edmond	18
McCurtain, Green	19
McCurtain, Ida *See* Jack & Jane Austin McCurtain	
McCurtain, Lucinda *See* Jack & Jane McCurtain	
McCurtain, Samuel	18
McDaniel, Tom	19
McEvery, May	19
McGilberry, Harris	18
McGilbry, James	18
McIntosh, John	19
McKinney, John	18
McKinney, Sampson	19
McKinney, Samuel	18
McKinney, Thompson	18
McKinney, Thompson-	18
McKinney, William H	*See* Mitanvbbi
McMurray, Nettie	19
Meah-to-ubbee	32
Meashia	37
Mea-sho-ste	34
Me-ayo-to-nah	36
Me-hah-tah-tah	34
Me-ha-to-na	36
Me-ha-to-nah	36
Me-haw	37
Me-heo-timah	29
Me-his-tubbee	35
Me-ho-nubbee	31
Melissa	30
Me-she-mah-tubbee	29
Meshum-tah-tubbee	34
Me-skambe	37
Me-ush-e-mah	30
Miashintvbi	26
Miash-tu-nah	30
Mihateka	27
Milaicha	26
Millard, B	18
Miller, Charles William	*See* Alnamvtvbbi
Miller, Daniel	18
Miller, Robert C	19
Mishaiontvbi	26
Mish-tubbee	29
Mocbb-be	29
Mockan-tubbee	32
Mohah	36
Mok-a-tubbee	30
Moncrief, Katie	19
Moncriff, William	18
Moore, Lyman	19
Morland, B	18
Morris, Abbie	19
Moses Dyer	26
Mosholetvbbi	18
Mo-wah-ho-nah,	30
Mulla-le-chubbee	33
Mush-shu-le-skak	31

N

Nail, Adam	17
Nail, Benjamin	17
Nail, Ethel	17
Nail, James	17
Nail, Joel H	17
Nail, John M	17
Nail, Joseph	17
Nail, Katie	17
Nail, Morris	17
Nail, Robert M	17
Nakhacho Humma	26
Nash, Sallie	17
Nelson, Brown	17
Nelson, Coleman E	18
Nice	*See*
Nitvkechi	17
Nocke-ne-hiah	32
Nock-ne-hiab	38

Nok-ho-ma-ho-yo	33
Nowah-ho-ka	33
Now-a-hoka	28
Nukhokla	25

O

Oakes, Lem	19
Oakes, Sue	20
Oakes, Thomas J.	19
Oaks, Daniel	19
Oanubbee	28
Oatha-che	34
Oka-in-chuch-mah	28
Okishtiah	29
Okishtish	29
Okis-te-no-nah	30
Ok-la-hah	34
Okla-me-ashab	34
Ok-le-mah-cheah-honah	34
Ok-le-mah-che-ah-honah	34
Oklimona's	25
Ok-lio-Oka	33
Ola-tubbee	32
Oliphant, Levi Carson	*See* Immakatvbbi
Olu-bbee-to-nah	32
Ona-hema	36
Onah-te-mah	34
Onah-tubbee	31
Oo-ne-tah-tah	*3*
Oon-tah-yubbee	37
Oo-yas-ke-wah-tah	1
Oshvn	26

P

Page, John	20, 37
Pah-ke-ti-mah	37
Panshiah-to-nah-mah	37
Parker, Gabe E.	20
Parshall, Lula	21
Pash-chubbee	37
Pate, Ella	21
Patterson, James	20
Pearle	5
Pe-as-tubbee	30
Pebworth, Emma	21
Perkins, David	20
Perkins, George	20
Perry, Andrew	20
Perry, Hardy	20
Perry, James	20
Perry, John	20
Perry, Joseph	20
Perry, W. C.	20
Peter	*4*
Phile-ah-hoyo	33
Pickens, Mary	21
Pickens, Solomon	20
Pis-a-hambe	28
Pisah-chish-e-mah	37
Pisah-Chubbee	31
Pisah-chum-tubbee	29
Pisah-honah	33
Pisah-ti-mah	33, 34
Pisambe	31
Pish-ho-timah	31
Pish-le-hubbee	31
Pish-no-ubbee	34, 35
Pish-te-she-mah	33
Piso-tubbee	37
Pitchlynn, A. C.	39
Pitchlynn, Alice	20
Pitchlynn, Charley	39
Pitchlynn, Ebenezer	20
Pitchlynn, Elizabeth C	39
Pitchlynn, John	20, 39
Pitchlynn, Josie	21
Pitchlynn, L. P.	20
Pitchlynn, Mary	39
Pitchlynn, Peter	20, 27, 39
Pitchlynn, Peter Perkins	20
Pitchlynn, Rhoda	39
Pitchlynn, Sariah	39
Pitchlynn, Silas	20, 39
Pitchlynn, Sophia F	39
Pitchlynn, Thomas J.	20, 39
Pitchlynn, William B.	20
Piyah-hoocta	35
Pohvbi	26
Polly	36
Pom-fillah	32
Pondexter, George	20
Ponok-to-chubbee	28
Pope, Alexander	20
Potah	33
Pots-le-chubbee	32
Pusley, Osborne	20
Pusley, Smallwood	21
Putte	32

R

Radford, Edmond	21
Raper Charles	2
Richard	5
Riddle, John	21
Riddle, Virginia	21
Riddle, William	21
Riley, James	21
Risner, Caroline	21
Risner, Carrie	21
Robb, David	21
Roebuck, William	*See* Zekiel Roebuck
Rolly Jones	26
Rosenthall, Ernestine	21

S

Sah-ne-co-yah	2
Sa-la-ruh	2
Salla	35
Sally	*3*, 36
Sampson	26
Saxton, Henry	21
Scott	5

Severs, Ambrose	21
Sexton, Martin	22
Seymour Baptis	27
Shampi-omah	37
Shampo-no-ka	30
Shatah,	30
She-ne-po-tubbee	29
Sherwood, Sophia	21
Shiwi	26
Shoney, Wilson	22
Sho-ti-mah	36
Simeon Hamilton	25
Simon Jone's	26
Si-yimo-hoka	29
Slowe Temah	35
Smallwood, Ben	21
Smallwood, William	21
Smith	2
Smith J L A	1
Solomon, Allen	21
Songster	1
Spring, Samuel	22
Spring, Samuel B	21
Stephen	25
Stephen Harrison Tvnvp	26
Stewart, Charles J	21
Stewart, William K	21
Stores, Richard Salter	22
Sul-te-she	*3*
Susan	1
Susy	2

T

Taafe, Maud	22
Taafe, May	22
Tah-ne-honah	34
Tah-nih	*3*
Take-uniye	36
Ta-la-tes-skih	*3*
Talo-moon-tubbee	34
Talowakvbi	27
Tamoah	33
Tanvp-aya	26
Tappan, Charles Long	*See* Oklushtvbbi
Tawantvbi	27
Taylor	27
Taylor, Ben	22
Taylor, Hudson	22
Taylor, Ida	22
Taylor, J	27
Taylor, Jones	22
Teah-ke-honab	30
Te-la-gus-kih	*3*
Telala	1
Temah	37
Te-mah	30
Temaka	36
Temalah	34
Temo-nah	33
Teni-yah-tubbee	36
Tennant, Carrie	22

Te-sa-ni-hih	2
Te-Sus-Ke Lucy	2
Thacker, Robert	22
Thomas	5
Thomas Howell	27
Thomas, Cleo	22
Thompson	26
Thompson, Ellis	22
Thompson, James	22
Thompson, Jane	22
Thompson, Joseph	22
Tick-ba-oonah	37
Tihlaiatvbi	27
Tiliki	26
Timonah	30
Tinson Eliza	1
Tinson H Clay	2
Tinson John C	1
Tinson Martha Jane	2
Tinson Nancy Ann	1
Tish-yo-tubbee	31
Tith-lo-ho-nah	32
Tombbee	37
Tonah	32
To-no-ho-ka	28
Tooka-chubbee	37
Trahern, George W	22
Trahern, James N	22
Trainer, L. B.	22
Tucker, Hampton	22
Tuk-a-lubbee	37
Tumbe	30
Turnbull, Florence	22
Turnbull, Lizzie	22
Turnbull, Turner B	22
Tush-ko-lutta	30

U

Ulth-la-honab	37
Una-ha-timab	36
Unte-cun-a-ubbee	30
Usray, Josephine	23
Usray, Josie	23

V

Vandever, Joseph	23
Vaughn, Loren D	23
Victor, Penson	23
Victor, Wilson	23
Vinson, Eliza	23

W

Wade, Alexander	23
Wade, Alfred	24
Wade, Jerry	24
Wade, John	23
Wade, Pickens	24
Wade, Simon	24
Wahington Hudson	*See*
Wahumma	26
Wakhumma, Sonny	27

Wales, Biza	23
Walker, Fay	23
Walker, George	23
Wall, David	23
Wall, James	27
Wallace	25, 35. *See*
Walls, Ida	23
Ward, Bessie	23
Ward, Nelson	23
Ward, Silas	23
Ward, Timothy	24
Ward, William	24
Washington, George H	23
Washington, George T	23
Wa-ti-nih	2
Weah-honah	34
Wea-honah	34
Webster, D. W.	23
Weirs, Andrew	24
Welch David	2
Welch Edward	2
Welch James	2
Welch Richard	2
Welch, A. C.	23
Wesley, Charles	24
Wesley, John	24
White, Joel	24
William	3, 5, 26
William, Alexander	24
William, Aries V.	24
William, Harris	24
William, Morris	24
William, Silvester	24
William, Soloman	24
Willis, Daisey	24
Willis, Simon P.	24
Wilson	25, 33
Wilson, Charles	23
Wilson, David	23
Wilson, Noah	24
Wilson, Sarah	24
Wilson, William P.	24
Woods, Simon	24
Wooley, Clara	23
Worcester, Samuel	24
Wright, Allen Jr.	25
Wright, Allen Sr	*See* Ishtimahelvbbi
Wright, Anna	25
Wright, Benjamin	24
Wright, Carrie	25
Wright, Dr. E. N.	25
Wright, Frank	25
Wright, James	25
Wyett, Jennie	24

Y

Yakohtambi	25
Yimab-knonab Kiyo-Kotubbee	28
Yimah-honab	29
Yim-me-tubbee	38
Yohab-to-nah	34
Yo-kome-timah	31
Yoko-temah	36
Yoko-tubbee	28
Yoniab-ho-anb	28
Yotah, Joshua	25
Yunetiah	30

www.ingramcontent.com/pod-product-compliance
Lightning Source LLC
LaVergne TN
LVHW081400060426
835510LV00016B/1919